UNBREAK MY HEART

MEETING MY CHILDREN AS STRANGERS

SUSAN MORROW

For permission requests, contact the publisher at:

HTA Books
High Touch Alliances
P.O. Box 140098
Dallas TX 75214-0098
Phone: +1 (214) 803-9769

ISBN: 0982286481
ISBN 13: 9780982286487
First Printing: November 2014
10 9 8 7 6 5 4 3 2 1
Library of Congress Control Number: 2014932096
HTA Books LLC, Dallas, TX

Dedication

To Monica and David, Always and Forever in My Heart

Acknowledgments

I always believed that one day I would write a book and share my story. When I was searching for Monica and David, friends and colleagues asked if I was going to do a book and I would say "someday." I knew that when I did, it had to feel right. There were moments after my children and I were reunited that I felt it was the time to start writing. Yet, I was not sure where to begin. I would write some snippets and thoughts. And, then something would pull me back from starting. My gut said no. About four years ago, the pieces began to fall into place. It was time.

First, I want to thank Darlene Ellison, Cynthia Stine, and everyone with HTA Books for all their superb efforts and work in bringing this book to fruition. A special appreciation to Darlene….I will never forget our first breakfast discussion and the momentum you provided to move my book project forward. Your encouragement and friendship are invaluable to me.

And to Gary Floyd, who captured my story in lyrics. You are an amazing individual with incredible talent. Thank you.

My very special gratitude to John and case managers with the National Center for Missing and Exploited Children who helped me in the search for my children. Words cannot express my profound appreciation for their belief in making my dream to reunite with Monica and David a reality. There are so many at the Center who I have had the privilege to get to know. They are all incredible people.

To Jose Luis, my attorney in Mexico, who went the extra mile in locating my children and making possible my reunion and initial visits with them. I will be eternally grateful to him, his lovely wife, Alejandra, and members of his firm.

My immense gratitude to all the law enforcement agencies and various non-profit, missing children's organizations, which helped in my search as well as Ron, my U.S. attorney and other legal counsel

To Abby, another searching parent, with whom I developed a special bond that will forever exist. I never thought I would find connections that were so vital to me.

To Kevin, my boss at the software company where I worked when Monica and David were abducted, my gratitude to him and his wife, Connie, for their support and belief that I could maintain my work responsibilities while searching for my children; to Anne, Duane and Sam, professional therapists and psychologists who have provided invaluable counseling and guidance; Roger and Brent, both of whom as ministers gave me spiritual insight; and business colleagues and clients to whom I am grateful for their support in my writing this book. A special thank you to Trista for developing my website and social media activities.

To my past, current, and forever special friends who have been there for and supported me as extended family, especially, Beth Ann; Linda; Andy; and Janet. To Janet W, my "big sister"...your love and support have been invaluable. You hold a special "forever" place in my heart. To Cheryl H., I so appreciate your ongoing encouragement for me to "keep writing."

A special tribute to Carolyn and Liz, both of whom departed this world too soon. Each made a lasting impact in my life; both are forever in my heart.

There are many other friends along with clients and acquaintances whom I have met along the way. I am immensely grateful for their support.

To my parents and sister, Cheryl, thank you for your own ways of support and affection.

And to Earl, my husband and best friend, who has been with me each step of this journey. This book would not have been possible without his incredible support, patience, and unconditional love. Above all, I dedicate this book to my precious children, Monica and David. Our bonds grow stronger each day.

One More Time

What a ride this has been
A stranger has become a friend
Where I end and you begin
One more time

To be patient, to be kind
Leave what's left behind, behind
Watching every hour unwind
Prove to you my love's not blind
One more time

Words by Gary Lynn Floyd, Songwriter and Composer

Table of Contents

Introduction · · · 1
Thanks for the Memories · · · 5
Anatomy of a Child Abductor · · · 11
Curse of the Amateur · · · 21
Where's A Policeman When You Need One? · · · 33
The Waiting Years · · · 45
Found! · · · 53
The Building Years · · · 67
The New Normal: Monica and David · · · 85
Monica's Story · · · 99
David's Story · · · 107
The New Normal: Susan and Earl · · · 113
Stories from the Kidnapped Files · · · 123
Appendix A: Cultural Differences
Between Mexico and The United States · · · 129
Appendix B: Challenges Getting Passports For The Children · · · 133
Appendix C: Resources for Families/
Volunteer Opportunities · · · 137
Appendix D: Combined Reflections · · · 139
About Susan Morrow · · · 149
Invite Susan to Speak to Your Group! · · · 153

Introduction

April 2, 1999

I paced in my client's lobby impatient and anxious. Every free moment I had, my mind wandered south to Mexico where my children were hidden from me. This week had been particularly endless, and now it looked like I would have to wait another week before hearing any news about the latest lead. I was hopeful and terrified at the same time. Twelve years of disappointments weighed heavily on my mind.

What if we'd made a mistake? What if these weren't my children? What if they were? Would they remember me? Were they as anxious to see me as I was to see them?

As the hot Dallas sun beat in the windows, my phone rang and I started to sweat. I answered the international call hardly able to speak. One of my Mexico attorneys, Lupita, was on the phone.

"I spoke with your daughter!" she joyously exclaimed.

At last the news I so desperately wanted! I cried into the phone from the depths of my soul. After the wave of emotion passed, Lupita told me more.

That was the good news. There was a complication. When she explained to my now-teenage daughter Monica that I'd looked for twelve years to find her and her brother David, she stammered, *"That's impossible! My mother is dead!"*

While you might think that I'm starting with the end of my story, it is the beginning. For the past 14 years since that day, I've built relationships with my beloved children from scratch. We were strangers to each other and now we are family. As my story will show, there is no "…and they lived happily ever after" when you finally reunite with your children. Creating a happy ending is a continuing process and journey. There are mistakes I made along the way that perhaps could have been avoided, and situations that brought us closer together.

For those who are still waiting to find their children or those who have just met them again for the first time, this is a love and hope story for you and your families. You can start over. You can connect with your children again. You can reclaim the family that was stolen from you. This new family won't match the fantasies and unarticulated expectations you undoubtedly have, but it can be something wonderfully different, loving and fulfilling.

When you read the parts written by my children in this book and see how far we've all come together, I hope it will help you as you create your "new normal" with your family.

I know you are doubtful, afraid and optimistic all at once. It is a mixture of feelings I lived with for many years. Over the twelve years, I felt despair. I had people tell me to give up – as if I could possibly give up a piece of my heart! I had been afraid this day would never come.

In a story full of shocks and surprises, I shouldn't have been surprised that my ex told the children I was dead, but I was. There is something so surreal about your partner and friend of many years kidnapping your children. Even after 12 years, it was incredible to me that he could be that kind of person and I never realized it until too late.

Twenty-six years later, I realize that I was not alone. Hundreds of thousands of family abductions occur every year; many of them are international. Today I reach out and support left-behind families to help them through the terrible waiting and then to reconnect with their children after the reunion.

There is such a big focus – and rightly so – on recovering the children, that few families think about what happens afterwards. How do you re-create your family with the strangers before you? When I finally saw Monica again she was 18 and David was 15. They had been told I was dead. And if I was not dead, where had I been? Why had I not tried to find them? To Monica and David, they were not missing; I was. It was a huge shock when I located them and not exactly a happy one because of all it implied about their father.

In the years since we were reunited, we've built a new family. It has taken more than a decade, but we feel like family to each other now. And for all the stress, sadness and struggle before and after reunification, it has been worth it to keep trying, to keep hoping, and to keep looking. My adult children, while they had never left my heart, are now back with me again and in my arms. I wrote this book to provide hope to the families who are still waiting, guidance for the families whose children have recently been abducted, and support for the very important work of rebuilding the family after the reunification.

Even when you know intellectually that you will be strangers to each other after a long separation, it is still shocking for parents. For the past years they've thought of hardly anything but their children. Their children may not have thought much about them at all. The warm reunion with hugs and tears may actually be a cool handshake and a neutral expression. Through my story, I'll explain how that happens and what to do about it. The reunion is just the beginning.

This book is not just for families with abducted children. Rebuilding a family applies to long-term separations and building relationships in a variety of situations including adoption, drug rehabilitation, imprisonment and more.

One

Thanks for the Memories

I threw open the front door and ran through the house calling out "Monica! David!" over and over again into the silent air. The panic that had begun the previous night when I could not reach my husband on the phone choked me. I was out of town on a business trip. On the immediate flight home I kept telling myself it was going to be OK. They'd be at home; my panic would be for nothing. I was overreacting. It was going to be OK, OK, OK, OK. "Oh God in Heaven, please make it OK!" I couldn't sit still in the plane, I couldn't drive home fast enough.

Standing in the middle of the house, the quiet was deafening. I went into my bedroom and sat on the bed when I spotted it: my husband's last message to me. I stared in astonishment at the words crudely and hastily scrolled in pink crayon on the bedroom mirror: "Thanks for nine years of memories."

My heart was pounding in my ears. I felt so shocked when the truth sunk in. This was no spontaneous trip with the kids to see his family. He wasn't coming back. The room, everywhere in the house was empty. So cold, so dark. Bags had been packed and taken. This could not be.

It must be a nightmare! My children were gone! Why on earth had my husband stolen them?! Why would he do this to me? I knew he wanted to return to Mexico one day but…this?!?

My incredible and beautiful babies who were part of me had been ripped from my arms and my heart. I had no idea where they were or how to reach them! I might never see them again!

What was I to do? Where was I to go? At age 37, I suddenly felt very old, without heart, without any meaning to my life. Fear penetrated the core of my being and I felt bloodless and lightheaded. How could I have been so deceived, betrayed, and naïve? How could I have left the kids at home with him? My mind ran around and around in circles. I blamed myself for not realizing what kind of person he was. In the next second I was sure I could talk to him and work everything out. I was terrified, angry and humiliated all at the same time. It was the worst moment of my life. My darkest day. I had failed to protect my children, and I didn't know what to do next.

David as a baby

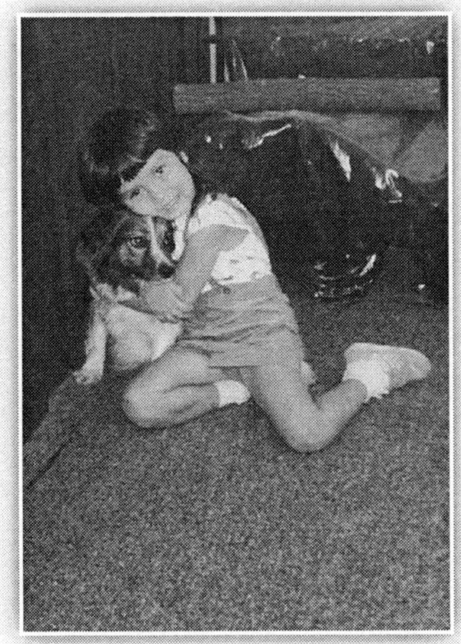

Monica before the abduction

Little did I know that I had just become a painful statistic. According to the National Center for Missing and Exploited Children®, the leading nonprofit organization in the U.S. that works with law enforcement, families and the professionals who serve them on issues related to missing and exploited children, over 200,000 family abductions occur each year.[1] And the majority of such abductions are in the U.S.

Back in 1987, I didn't know how many other parents knew my pain. This was pre-internet and pre-cable. I was not aware of any organizations to turn to for help. I thought I was on my own to figure this out, and I made mistakes on the way. In the many years since Monica and David were taken from me, more awareness of the problem and more resources for grieving families left behind have become available. Even so, nothing can prepare you for the devastation of having your children taken from you. If the fleeing parent takes them outside the United

1 National Center for Missing and Exploited Children, www.ncmec.org

States, it can be very difficult to get support from other governments even with agreements in place between the U.S. and certain countries.

Even if they are still in the U.S., it can be very hard to track them down. It will likely cost a lot of money to search for your children and can be particularly crippling if the leaving parent was the earner for the family. It is almost equally as crippling when the searching parent was the earner. Sometimes not all of the children in the family are taken, so you have shocked, traumatized children at home too. In the beginning you'll be hopeful of a quick resolution. For some there is a happy ending with a quick recovery. For parents like me, however, it can be a very long time.

The very good news is that the majority of parents left behind do locate and/or reunite with their children at some point. In cases like mine, it may be much later when they are older teenagers or young adults, but it happens.

Today I support families with missing children through various national missing children's organizations. I've held hands and prayed with many distraught parents and family members. I've helped them start to rebuild their relationships with their estranged children. What I've learned from their experiences has been woven into this book also.

While my focus and experience is with family abductions, the difficult task of building a family with older children is faced by parents with adopted children, in addition to those parents whose children have been stolen by strangers. Many people will clap you on the back and congratulate you when you find your children or adopt an older child, but they will have no clue how to help you or support you when you try to parent your kids and build a relationship. It can be a very isolating experience. Traditional parenting rules do not apply here.

As this book was nearing completion, three kidnapped teenage girls were rescued from years of terrible abuse by a stranger. While the media and their families rejoiced at their escape and recovery, my first thought was "Oh my God. I hope the parents are up for this."

As a parent you hope and pray and plead every day for the return of your child and there is a kind of magical thinking that takes place that says, "Everything will be OK when I get them back." Only it isn't. There is still a lot of work ahead. The reality that there is no end to human suffering can be crushing for some families. The reality that their children have been damaged by what happened to them – even if there is no abuse – is overwhelming for parents already consumed by grief for their children and guilt over not preventing this from happening or from not finding them sooner…believe me. I know a lot about sadness and irrational guilt.

I've learned that it takes a long time for kids to grapple with what happened to them, particularly since the abducting parent is still dad or mom. They aren't out of the picture even though you have your kids back. Many children taken by strangers form a bond with them that is difficult to unravel later. With the children of family abductors, the bond is already there and may be strengthened in the other parent's absence. The abductor may tell them the other parent is dead or doesn't want them anymore. They often try to estrange the children from the other parent to justify their own behavior and to make them look better in comparison. Children who are parentally abducted are the true victims. They are caught in the middle as they love both parents.

The purpose of this book is not to depress parents and families, but to hold out a realistic picture of how it can happen. You can get your kids back - hearts and minds. You can be a family again, but it is easier if you leave your expectations at the door and realize it will require patience and work. There is so much I wish I had known from the beginning. My hope for you is that you can avoid my mistakes and find the strength it will take to reunite and rebuild your family.

It is possible. It is worth it. Hang in there.

Two

Anatomy of a Child Abductor

What does a family abductor look like exactly? He or she looks just like you and your family. This is part of what is so bizarre to the parents left behind. Here is someone they thought they knew, someone they loved who is now the cruelest person they've ever met.

Child abductors cross all classes, races, genders and cultures. Women are on par with men for abductions. Over the past few years, I've seen more men than women being left behind - particularly with the rise of stay-at-home dads. Any family can be affected. Some of the reasons why abductions are growing include the increasing rate of divorces and tough economic times. The abducting parent may be involved in other illegal activities and is undeterred by the fact that she or he is committing a crime.

The parent may be an abuser who wants privacy with the children although that is not as common as people fear. Often the children are taken in revenge against the other parent. Whatever the reason, one thing is consistent among abductors: they are not thinking about their children's well-being. They see them as possessions and tools. They don't see or care that the child is mourning the other parent. They minimize and justify the impact their behavior will have on their abandoned spouse and the children.

As you will see from my own story, the searching parent often unintentionally enables the abductor. They will sometimes wait to inform the authorities or to ask for help because they are hopeful they can get the kids back or resolve the problem by themselves. Many mistakenly assume "no one will believe me," or that the police won't give it much attention because the children were abducted by a parent rather than a stranger. Sadly, there are some law enforcement officials that still consider parental/family abductions as domestic cases.

Ironically, the parent left behind *IS* thinking about the children. They will be lenient with the other parent for the sake of the kids. They are concerned that if they call the authorities, the other parent will go to jail which will be traumatizing to the kids. They may believe that being compliant with the abductor's wishes will insure the safety of the children and/or secure the opportunity to see them again. They may also believe that they will reconcile with the abducting parent one day in spite of the fact that she/he stole the children and left them. They may think this is a rough patch in their marriage rather than the crime it truly is. Often the searching parent is wracked with guilt and grief, and paralyzed by indecision and fear. They may be reeling from the shock and full of denial.

For these reasons and many more, they may wait to call on law enforcement which means that the trail becomes cold. They may wait to call family and friends for support, which isolates them further and makes the experience even more miserable. They may try to recover the kids themselves and make the situation even worse because they are amateurs.

I know that was true in my case. I couldn't believe that my husband would do that to me, to our family, to the kids. I made up all kinds of justifications for why he would take the kids to Mexico while I was out-of-town on business. He said the terrible things he said because he was angry. He would cool down…my denial drive was rolling in full gear. Until I saw that note on the mirror, I still had hope that it was somehow all a bad dream or a marital fight we could fix. That was more than 24 hours after he was in Mexico with our children.

With the benefit of hindsight, I realize that I'd been in denial for some time. There were signs even from the beginning of our relationship that Carlos (not his real name) wasn't a stand-up guy.

In 1977, I was living in Cuernavaca, Mexico when I met Carlos. I had been asked to teach an English class to executives at Chesebrough-Ponds. Carlos sat in the front row. He was affable, interacted with others in the class and had a strong command of the language. I liked his personality and air of confidence.

Carlos would watch me while I taught the lessons. He seemed to capture every word and would always smile at me every chance that he had. I was flattered and enchanted. We began to talk after class. As the class sessions progressed, so did my after class conversations with Carlos and we began to spend social time together.

In the meantime, I accepted an offer from an import-export company in Mexico City to work in sales. Shortly afterwards, Carlos left me a message that he had accepted a marketing management position with another American company, Warner Lambert, based in Mexico City. We connected. Carlos shared that he was ready to move forward. The more we talked, the more we agreed that a move together to Mexico City would allow us to develop and strengthen our relationship.

In early 1981, I learned that I was pregnant. I was not sure how Carlos would feel about being a father again since he did not spend much time with his daughter from his previous marriage. In hindsight, that was another clue that I missed - his perspective on children. Our families' reactions to my pregnancy were mixed. Carlos' family was happy for us. His mother, in particular, seemed more approving of me than previously. This was more than likely due to Latin cultural mores of having children.

My parents were not happy, not because they did not like me to have a baby, but because they were concerned about my relationship with Carlos. At the time, I did not understand this. All I felt then was disappointment, abandonment and rejection. Yet, I was not surprised. My parents, even my sister, had never approved of my going to Mexico originally. They did not understand; most importantly, they never tried. Other American families would visit while their children lived/worked in Mexico. Mine never did, so I rejected their concern about Carlos since I felt they had rejected me.

Carlos was spending more time at the office and often did not get home until late at night. He also started to travel more and was not communicative about his trips and what they entailed. When he was in town, Carlos would get together with office "buddies" for happy hours or similar gatherings usually about once a week and never let me know when he would be home. When he did arrive home at 2:00 or 3:00 a.m., he was usually drunk. I told myself it was a cultural thing, that this was what Mexican men did, and not a problem with our relationship. For many women, these various signs would have come to a "three strikes, you're out" moment. But, I was lonely and pregnant.

As the time drew closer to my due date, I wanted to reconnect and I met him at a conference he was attending in San Diego. We went dancing and had a good time, but there was still a gnawing, uneasy feeling inside me.

At my office, the owners, Anthony and Barbara, saw that something was not right. They were a bi-cultural couple. Anthony was a U.S. citizen and Barbara was born and grew up in Mexico. One day Anthony expressed his and Barbara's heartfelt concern. They felt that I should not remain in Mexico for the birth. Carlos was not someone, they felt, who would take care of me and my baby. We would be far better in the U.S. away from the relationship I was in. Anthony said he would arrange for me to fly to Texas the next day even that evening, if possible, and go to a hospital there.

I was stunned with his offer and so appreciative that he and Barbara wanted to help me. We agreed that I would let him know the next day.

Looking back now I recognize that if outsiders are expressing concern about your marriage or your spouse, they are probably right! It takes so much personal concern to overcome people's natural reticence to get involved, that if someone outside your family says something to you about your partner, take it as a red flag worthy of consideration.

Unfortunately, Anthony's offer was not to be realized. I was not feeling well when I awoke the next morning. Carlos had gone to work and I could not reach him. His brother Ramon took me to the hospital where I had an emergency C-section. I remember very little until I awoke. Carlos appeared by my bed and said that we had a beautiful daughter, Monica, born at 4:33 p.m. December 18, 1981.

All I could think was, "Where in the hell have you been?" But I was optimistic that his behavior would be different now that he was a father. I know now what a mistake it is to think this way. If anyone can learn from my mistakes, I will be so pleased.

The first six months were peaceful, compatible and joyful. Carlos was more attentive at first. My time was focused on Monica. She was a wonderful and easy baby. She loved being outdoors and also loved cuddling on my lap while I would read to her. I had such beautiful dreams and plans for her and our family.

On weekends, Carlos and I would take her bicycling with us or on other outdoor activities. A familial thread seemed to strengthen within and he enjoyed spending time – just the three of us. Even our time together was better. When Carlos' mother offered to take care of Monica, we would have dates. We would go to the Zona Rosa in downtown Mexico City and have a drink or coffee at an outside café. Other times we would go to dinner, a movie, or dance occasionally at a local club.

I went back to work part-time to help with expenses. In July 1982, things began to get bumpy. Mexico experienced a sharp economic downturn and Warner Lambert downsized Carlos' job.

I will never forget when Carlos picked me up from work that day. He was with his brother, Ramon, who was driving. They had both been drinking. I was scared both from their behavior and from being in a car with an intoxicated driver. I finally convinced them to stop the car so that we could talk.

As I had always thought that Carlos had a good relationship with his boss, I was frankly puzzled that he had not offered to place him in another position. Carlos said that they had discussed a few possibilities; however, only one position was available and it would require a significant drop in pay and title. He was not willing to do this.

This was one of many examples of Carlos' pride getting in the way of what needed to be done. His image of himself, the kind of person he perceived himself to be, was more important than the needs and feelings of others, including his new baby and wife. While this is one of many examples that I had of this truth, I ignored it. I justified and explained away his behavior to myself because I did not want to see it.

Carlos' severance package helped for several months. He began to job search, but companies were not hiring. Carlos was frustrated, yet kept insisting that sooner or later he would find a job that was parallel to the one he had had at Warner Lambert. He was not willing to take less.

We agreed that I would have to find a full-time position at least until he had a job. In the end I found two part-time positions – an assistant with a financial services firm and the other with a U.S. attorney who needed document translations. The income from both jobs only marginally helped us. It was a stressful time.

Carlos was not happy. He wanted to give up on the job search. In January 1983, we moved to Dallas. I knew that I would never return, but Carlos saw our move as temporary until the economy improved in Mexico.

Once again, I was hoping that things would change. I imagined him getting a good job in the U.S. and wanting to stay. In this fantasy thinking I disregarded the strong cultural pull he felt to Mexico, his family ties and his many resources there. Many families with whom I've worked had a similar dynamic. The abducting parent wanted to go home and take his/her children back too.

I worked temp jobs while I searched for a full-time job. I landed with a non-profit organization about three months later. Shortly after that, I was contacted by a public relations firm offering me a position that would pay twice the salary I was making. It was an exciting time for me, but not for Carlos.

Carlos finally received his work permit and proceeded to look for employment. I encouraged him to engage with an executive search firm and acquaint them with his skills and background experience working with large U.S. firms in Mexico. He found a couple of opportunities with smaller companies and although the positions were more office management or sales related, they afforded income. However, both of these jobs were short-term. Carlos had difficulties with his boss or did not meet the position's expectations.

This job discontent was another red flag that Carlos did not intend to stay. I was supporting our family and received more and better job offers that ensured I would stay. Carlos did not like me working even though he couldn't keep a job himself. I had to travel sometimes for work and Carlos had to watch Monica. David was born in 1986.

At last in October 1987, Carlos was presented with a job opportunity at NCH Corporation in Dallas, one of its worldwide offices. He moved quickly through the interviewing process and became the preferred candidate for the position. As the final step prior to being offered the position, Carlos told me that he had to meet with one of the senior vice presidents in Mexico City, one of the company's liaisons with whom he would be working in his new position in Dallas.

I was excited and happy for him – at long last, he would be professionally content once again, to say nothing of how much this would mean for our family financially. The interview date coincided with a trade show in Las Vegas I was attending for my company. Carlos decided that while he was in Mexico City, he would see his family for a few days. A close friend agreed to take care of Monica and David for the few days we were both out of town.

I left for the trade show on Sunday, November 1, 1987. Carlos was to leave on Monday, November 2 and would take the children to our friend Ann's home early that morning before catching his plane. The next day I found an urgent message waiting for me from Ann when I returned to my hotel. Ann was beside herself with fear. Carlos had called her early Monday morning to say that his flight had been delayed to Monday evening and that he would take Monica to school and pick her up. He would keep David with him and then bring both children to Ann's after school. Carlos never showed up.

Ann called the school and was told that Monica had not come – her father had called to say that she was sick. Ann called the police; however, she was told that they could not help her – no one was considered missing until 48 hours and the children were with their father.

In a trembling, hysterical panic I started calling Carlos' family members in Mexico City. I finally talked with his sister-in-law who let me talk to Carlos. He said that the children were his and needed to be with him. Crying, begging, and pleading with him only made him angry. Carlos hung up the phone. My body was overwhelmed with anger and rage. I'm sure my hurt and screams could be heard all over Las Vegas. I had been betrayed on every level imaginable. My heart felt like it had been ripped from my body.

The next morning I left Las Vegas living a nightmare that I prayed would evaporate when I awoke. I would go home and the children would be there. While it sounds crazy now, many parents of kidnapped children have experienced the same kind of irrational, hopeful denial. The horror and immensity of the truth is hard to take. Arriving in Dallas, I saw the writing on the mirror and reality sunk in. My nightmare was just beginning.

Not surprisingly, I learned that Carlos had never had an interview scheduled with NCH in Mexico City. There was no such final interviewing process – the company was already going to offer him the position! His success at finding a job was the trigger that made him decide to leave.

This is also pretty common. I've talked with many parents who had experienced economic hardships and whose spouse wanted to go home where he/she felt in control and where there were resources and contacts that could be applied. As you can see from Carlos' initial response to me, his children were his property. This is the prevailing mindset of most abductor parents. While *he* was obviously indispensable to his children, their mother was not and could be easily replaced by other women. (I've seen the opposite sentiment from women abductors – the father is unimportant, etc.)

This is the clearest indication that the abductor will not give the children back. They are not sorry for the pain they are causing, they don't feel badly for their children, and they feel entitled. At this point, only an outside force can intervene. I didn't know that, so I spent futile time trying to negotiate with Carlos for the children.

You may be reading this chapter and thinking, "a lot of people are jerks like this and they never abduct their children!" And it is true. Child abduction is an extreme act. It is virtually impossible to determine if someone is a child abductor before they do it. There was no way I could have reasonably expected or known that Carlos would do this despite his bad behavior to me. However, I still blame myself for not getting out of the relationship sooner. I share this part of my story in the hopes that if someone sees signs like these in their relationship, he/she will consider getting out even if there are no children involved. A liar is still a dangerous person.

Three

Curse of the Amateur

There is a reason why people shouldn't represent themselves in court. Neither should they try to execute the job of law enforcement, negotiate with their abductors or do any job for which they are not specifically trained. The curse of the amateur is far more prevalent than the success of the amateur. The rare successes make great "made-for-TV" movies. The failures agonize in private over the loss of their children and their *additional* failure to protect them.

The parent is in emotional shock and upheaval and desperately needs an outside voice and partner to think through the situation clearly. One of the first mistakes I made in the aftermath was not to reach out for help. I should have had someone less emotionally involved sitting with me in meetings with law enforcement and lawyers, to think through things reasonably. I told people, of course, but I didn't take their help. Big mistake.

I was in a daze, shock. I went on auto-pilot. I knew I had to do something. I needed to call someone or ones. Who first? I have no idea who I called first, or second, or even tenth, but I remember that I did not want to talk with anyone. I did not want anyone to know. Particularly, my parents. Why? For one thing, I was sure that I could resolve the situation. In a week or two, Monica and David would be home. Crisis solved. Bad dream gone. For another, I was afraid I would get judged and criticized for letting this happen. Others would know I was a bad parent who failed to protect her kids. It would be much easier to tell my story once the children were home safely and I had redeemed myself. This kind of irrational thinking is very common among parents of kidnapped children, which is why it would have been so helpful to have had a sane person helping me out in those early days. I needed someone who cared but was not freaking out themselves. The importance of reaching out and soul searching for the appropriate individual/individuals to help is paramount. In addition, today there are support organizations that understand abduction/missing children and help those going through crises.

Ultimately I called a few close friends, the Richardson, Texas Police Department, an attorney in Dallas, Monica's teacher, her soccer coach, etc. I learned from my attorney that I had to obtain divorce and child custody agreements before I could bring Monica and David back to the U.S. Further, I needed to have an attorney to represent me in Mexico. Even though I would have a divorce and potential sole custody of Monica and David, the Mexican attorney would need to pursue charges in Mexico, serve Carlos with papers, and present to a Mexican court for a judge's ruling. My attorney Ron located a contact in Mexico City who agreed to help.

During this time, I became more hopeful. I would get a divorce and get my kids back. Simple, right? I was convinced that I had to make a trip to Mexico alone. I believed that the only way I was ever going to have Monica and David with me was to reason with Carlos. I was determined. Most of all, I needed and had to see Monica and David. Seeing my children would make everything OK. The nightmare would disappear. Necessary legal documents were one thing, but being with my children was all that mattered. I could do this. Carlos was my husband.

I knew him. I knew how to talk with him. The curse of the amateur had taken hold.

For my first trip, I stayed with Anna Marie, a friend whom I had met while living in Mexico. My local attorney, Alberto Gonzales, explained how Mexican family court worked, but my thoughts were on seeing my children again, so I barely paid attention. He expressed concern about my safety and recommended that I meet with Carlos in a public place. He went with me just in case.

It was surreal. On the one hand, Carlos was my husband who had never hit me or tried to hurt me physically, but he had also stolen my children. Was it too far a stretch to think he might hurt me to get me to back off? The answer to that question was "No!" It was a very reasonable conclusion made by an attorney who had seen it happen. While it may be very difficult to think that the abducting spouse could be dangerous, it is vital to your continuing safety. I was glad I had Mr. Gonzales with me.

When I finally connected with Carlos at his mother's home, I was surprised and relieved that he agreed to meet at a well-known restaurant. I was concerned at the same time. Mr. Gonzales' comments regarding my safety kept echoing.

The closer the time came for me to meet Carlos, the greater the rage and hatred I felt. I had to keep reminding myself I had one motive and that was to see and bring Monica and David home. Once I saw Carlos, I instantly felt cold and calm. This was for the children.

My meeting with Carlos was short. I do not remember much of the conversation except that he said he would maybe bring Monica and David to visit. He said nothing about them going home with me. Knowing he was trying to provoke me, I kept calm and asked him to please bring Monica and David to see me the next day.

When he agreed, I felt hopeful. I had made progress. I could do this. I was ignoring the fact that Carlos had all the power and leverage. He was in his home country with his children. This was a game to him – one in which he wanted me to go away and leave him alone.

When I arrived back at Anna Marie's home, I shared my day with her and her husband Antonio. They said the right things; however, they were not comfortable. The body language was all wrong. I was disheartened. I could tell they wanted me to go. The support I had hoped to receive from them was not there. I felt lonely.

The next day, I counted the hours. Carlos had said he would come by early afternoon. About 1:30, he arrived without the children. I could not believe it! Rationally I should not have been surprised or upset. Why should Carlos keep his promise when he had already betrayed and lied many times over? I pressed to see the children.

He decided not to bring them because he knew I would not be content with just a visit. I wanted to take them back to Dallas. After saying repeatedly that I just wanted to see Monica and David, Carlos finally said OK, he would bring them. In fact, he said, he would "allow" me to take David home. If I agreed to that, he would just bring David!

The implications of that statement shocked me to the core. It was a terrible thing for him to do. I didn't know what to say. My heart was aching more than ever. Somehow, though, I had to keep a window open to communicating with Carlos. It was the only way to have any contact with Monica and David.

To buy myself some time, I said yes to Carlos' proposition. We arranged for him to bring David the following morning. I begged Carlos to bring Monica too.

I made plans to return to Dallas the afternoon of the following day. This way I could tell Anna Marie and Antonio I was leaving and would have David with me. My hope of all hopes was, of course, that I would have both children to take home to Dallas.

Of course, he did not come. Two hours late, Carlos called. He said that something had come up and he was unable to bring the children. In fact, he said, the more that he had thought about it, he decided he would not bring them at all. David was definitely not going to go home with me, and, neither would Monica. Nor was I to see either of them!!

I slammed the phone down. I was shaking. What should I do? After a long cry and a walk, I decided that the best thing I could do was to go back to Dallas and obtain help. I was alone in Mexico with no support. I needed guidance.

In hindsight, this play of events was predictable. As an amateur negotiator, I did not understand Carlos' position or what he wanted at all. Nor did I understand my position. I had no leverage with him. My begging and crying (nor staying calm for that matter) hadn't changed his mind – it merely told him that he was being successful with his plan to get rid of me. His obscene offer of only taking David was meant to shock me. His refusal to bring them the next day was to put me in my place and remind me of his power. He wanted me to feel helpless so I'd give up without too much inconvenience to him.

It was now December, more than a month since Monica and David had been abducted and more than two weeks since I had made the first trip to Mexico.

In that time, I had spoken with my attorneys and local law enforcement, and surrounded myself with support from friends. I had also gone back to work, which was comforting in more ways than I could have imagined. Everyone was incredibly supportive.

I finally told my parents about the abduction. They were upset and wanted to help. They wanted to stay continually in touch. They were angry that I waited so long to tell them. I learned years later how really devastated both Mom and Daddy were, particularly my father. At the time, I could only think about getting Monica and David back, but family abductions hurt the extended family too.

The holidays were quickly approaching. While I was pursuing a divorce and sole custody per the advice of both my attorneys in Dallas and Mexico, I had made no progress in reaching a solution to bring both children home.

I missed Monica and David more than ever. I closed the door of Monica's bedroom and put David's crib in there so I would not have to look at any items belonging to both children. My heart would ache every time I saw their clothes, their toys and beds. All I could do was cry and sometimes scream.

I had a few brief conversations with Carlos. When I was in Dallas, he was comfortable in talking. I was not a threat to him. Why did he agree to talk? Perhaps Monica kept asking about me. He may have also been thinking that I would agree to come to Mexico and stay. He might or could have agreed for me to come to Mexico in order to arrange for something to happen to me if I did not behave. "Accidents" have happened to other parents.

Not knowing what else to do and unable to stop myself from trying, I kept calling. I told him that I wanted to see Monica and David for Christmas in Mexico. He agreed and even though he'd lied to me before, I grasped to the straw of hope. I bought gifts and thought that maybe the nightmare would end with this trip.

Everyone else in my life was worried. They made me promise to keep in touch and let them know when I arrived. As 1987 was before cell phones, email, and the Internet, long-distance communication was much more challenging and expensive.

I left for Mexico early the morning of December 25. This time I made reservations at a hotel near downtown Mexico City. I had a desperate and unrealistic plan: if I could be with Monica and David alone, I would get to the airport and leave the country with them before Carlos found out.

He arrived earlier than I expected. Monica was so excited to see me. She ran and hugged me. I didn't want to let her go and neither did she. David ran over to me and put his head on my lap. He knew though he didn't talk yet that I was his "Mama," and he wanted to give me all the love he had to give.

My plan had been for both Monica and David to stay with me. Carlos said he would have dinner with us, and then leave us until the next morning.

The visit was so bizarre while Carlos was around. Monica and David opened their gifts and had fun playing with them. I also joined in the fun all the while thinking about the best way to leave the hotel once Carlos left.

I did not want Carlos to have dinner with us. It was uncomfortable to be with him, yet at the same time I did not want to arouse his suspicion. I tried to think of ideas that might work.

Shortly before dinner, he left for a few moments to get restaurant recommendations from the concierge. While he was gone, I moved his backpack off a chair. It was heavy. I looked inside and there was a revolver!

I realized that Carlos' reason to leave the room was a test to see what I might do with the children. Any move I made to leave the hotel with Monica and David would be dangerous for all of us. I needed assistance; however, who was I to call? My attorney in Mexico was on vacation for the holidays. There was no one else in Mexico City I could trust. I wanted to call friends, contacts in the U.S. Again, though, how would they be able to help? How foolish I was not to have planned my trip better! I could have asked a friend to come with me even if he or she stayed in another hotel. I was experiencing the curse of the amateur in full force.

Nevertheless, I was in the situation, and I had to focus on what I could do. When we later left for the restaurant, I could not help but glance at the backpack Carlos carried with him. I had never felt so nervous and scared!

I stayed focused on Monica and David during the meal and kept framing their beautiful faces in my mind. Carlos talked about some of the news of the day in Mexico and the difficulties the government was having with drug offenders, etc. I did not quite get why he went into such detail until he mentioned those being arrested, including foreign citizens, and how a Mexican jail was not a good place to be, particularly for women. Ah, right. It was a threat.

When we returned to the hotel, Carlos left. I did not know what to do. I feared that he had not left the hotel. I decided to conduct a test and took Monica and David downstairs to the gift shop. I had an excuse ready, but he was neither in the lobby nor anywhere else inside the hotel. I thought about asking the clerk at the front desk about a taxi to take us to the airport but decided to return to the room to think first.

We had been in the room only a few minutes when Carlos knocked on the door. He said he had lost a key he needed and thought he might have left it in the room. Of course! He had spies at the hotel. I felt incredibly naïve for not predicting that and having a plan in place to counter it. After he left again, any thoughts I had to leave the hotel vanished.

I held on to the children all night and the next day and through the next afternoon as Carlos took me to the airport. My heart was breaking. My brain was screaming at the same time. I needed help. I had to survive. If something happened to me, Monica and David would never have their mother hold them again.

Monica cried out "please don't go!" I had tears tasting like salt coming down my face. Never had any words I had ever said meant more, "I promise with all my heart I will BE BACK!"

I didn't see them again for 12 years.

Reflections

With these two trips I learned difficult lessons that I use today to help the families I support. While some of these ideas seem obvious, as you can tell from my story, a distraught parent is not in their right mind.

- **Never go alone** – Find an ally that is not emotionally invested the way you are. Take them with you for support to meetings with law enforcement and any meetings with the other parent. Have plans in place for your safety and the children's.

- **Provide itinerary and detailed information to family and friends** – I never told my parents about the abduction until after I returned from the first trip. While I had legal matters/ proceedings in action, e.g., scheduled meetings with my attorney in Mexico, initial documents to pursue divorce/custody, I neglected to disclose my trip plans with close friends and family members. If something had happened to me in Mexico, my family and friends would not have known where to begin to look for me or get help for me.

- **Resist magical thinking** – This is the hardest lesson because you are so broken-hearted and desperate, but a family abduction is very real and requires detailed planning and implementation to resolve. Being naïve is a form of denial. For me this was a way to survive the initial impact of my children being abducted, but it did not help me get them back and I put myself into dangerous situations.

- **Understand the abductor's agenda** – Abductors want you to go away and leave them alone with the children. Appealing to their better nature, trying to make them feel guilty or sorry for you or to even regret taking the children in the first place is naïve. These kids are theirs and they are entitled. You do not matter to the kids the way they do. Your planning and strategies will be more effective if you keep this in mind.

- **Understand what makes you/made you a perfect target** – There are common characteristics among abandoned spouses from before the abduction. Many were isolated and lonely when they met their spouse – perhaps living in another country like me. Many don't have strong family ties. This makes an ideal situation for abductors because they know the person left behind won't have a lot of support and resources to pursue the children. You will have to overcome these issues as part of the process of recovering your children.

- **Understand that a liar lies** – Carlos had lied to me repeatedly before and during our marriage, and yet I stayed with him. After he took the children he continued to lie to me and I still hoped that he was telling me the truth! That was the desperate mother in me, but all it did for me was feed into the magical thinking.

- **Listen to outside perspectives** – I had friends, my bosses at work, my family and others all telling me that they did not trust Carlos to have my best interest at heart. I regret not listening to them. I regret that I was too defensive to see that they did have my best interests at heart.

- **Know you cannot change him/her** – This was a mistake I made in my marriage. I kept thinking he would change, that things would be different, that having a baby would make things different, moving to Dallas would make things different. While this wishful fantasy is common in many relationships, it can be dangerous if you are dealing with deceitful, selfish and controlling behaviors. If your spouse is vain and prideful, if he/she seems indifferent to you, if his/her needs come before yours, you need to leave. He/she will not change.

- **Don't underestimate cultural issues** – I gave little weight to the cultural differences between the United States and Mexico. I had adjusted to living in Mexico, how hard would it be for Carlos to adjust to the U.S.? I was naïve enough to think he might even like it better! This was a bit of cultural prejudice on my part, and it meant I missed the big red flags that he would be going back to Mexico sooner rather than later.

- **Get counseling for yourself** – Carlos comes from a culture that sees counseling as a weakness in certain aspects, so I would have never gotten him to go; however, I strongly wish I had sought out counseling for myself long before he took the children. In the years since, I've worked through a lot of issues. Counseling has helped me survive the tough years without my children, the long search, and the dynamics of my marriage so I didn't have to repeat them with my current husband. If your children have been abducted, don't try to go this alone! You need all the help you can get, including emotional support from a professional.

- **Get family support** – With some families this may not be possible, but if you can mend fences and rally the family around you, this is the time. Carlos had a fairly large family in Mexico which supported him in myriad ways from money to babysitting to helping him get a job to giving him a place to stay and much more. Plus there is all the emotional support a family provides. I did not have that kind of support for a long time so I had to build it. It makes a difference. I see a lot of situations where searching parents have no money, no job, few resources and a distant family. They are not in a position to pursue the abductor financially or emotionally. This is a situation where family support can make a huge difference.

Four

Where's A Policeman When You Need One?

In 1987, available resources for parents who experienced family abductions were limited at best. There was no Internet to Google information. Communications technology was in its infancy. I did not know anyone who had a missing child, much less who had experienced a family abduction. I had read or heard on the news about children being abducted by strangers; however, I had never thought about it other than to feel sad for the families. I did not know who to contact for help other than my attorney, law enforcement, and the U.S. State Department.

The concept of family abduction was not understood at the time Monica and David were abducted, even though its occurrence was increasing due to custody battles incurred through divorce. Parental abduction was not considered a crime; it was a domestic issue. Law enforcement was not willing to become involved unless there was reason to believe the children were in physical danger. Even today, in spite of more awareness and education, family abduction is still not understood completely and, I suspect, never will be.

As is still true today, if law enforcement did not have the legal documentation, officials were unable to pursue a missing child if abducted by the other spouse. In situations where a custody order had been violated, local and state police had the jurisdiction needed to help locate the child, although their willingness to engage was sporadic. The same was true for the FBI.

In my case, I had no legal documents at the time Monica and David were abducted. While a local police officer, David S., at the Richardson Police Department was empathetic and wanted to help, he did not know what to do or where to turn. He reported the children to the Texas State Clearinghouse for Missing Children. I provided photos, which the Clearinghouse posted. Other than that, the police officer suggested that I contact my Dallas attorney, which I had already done, the U.S. State Department, and U.S. Embassy in Mexico City.

The complexity of my situation was enhanced due to Carlos taking the children to his native country. As we were legally married at the time of the abduction, he had committed no crime either here in the U.S. or in Mexico.

Today, family abduction is a crime in every state, although individual state criminal laws vary widely. Under state law, family abduction is described by a variety of names including custodial interference, custody deprivation, child stealing and parental kidnapping.[2]

The basic elements in the state crime of family abduction are typically the wrongful taking or retention of a child in violation of a court order or other law, without a valid defense to make the conduct legal. In many cases, it is a felony offence that carries a jail sentence. The National District Attorney's Association's website, www.ndaa.org, provides a comprehensive summary of state criminal custodial interference laws under Parental Kidnapping Statutes.

2 The National Center for Missing and Exploited Children (NCMEC), http://www.missingkids.com/LegalResources/Domestic

There is currently a federal law that prohibits law enforcement agencies from establishing or maintaining a waiting period before accepting a missing child report (42 U.S.C. §5780). Federal law requires law enforcement agencies to respond in a specific way, regardless of the reason a child is missing. It is not necessary for parents or guardians to have a custody determination to report a child missing to law enforcement. However, a parent typically is encouraged to obtain this because a custody order can help clarify and define rights and responsibilities and obtain the assistance of law enforcement for the pickup and return of the child. Parents or guardians should ask law enforcement to enter information about their child into the FBI's National Crime Information Center database.

Today, one of the leading organizations to help locate and return missing children is the National Center for Missing and Exploited Children, www.ncmec.org. The National Center was launched in 1984, three years before Monica and David were abducted. At the time of their abduction, I was not aware of the organization. Thankfully, I discovered the National Center in 1990. It would be through the National Center's attention and focus that I located my children.

According to the National Center, parents are urged to do the following if their child or children have been abducted:[3]

1) Contact your local law enforcement agency.

2) Call the National Center at 1-800-843-5678. There are case management teams which provide technical assistance and support for families, law enforcement agencies, and attorneys. They assist in the location and recovery of missing children nationally and internationally. The family abduction case managers work each case individually, coordinating with government and non-governmental agencies in the U.S and other countries regarding both civil and criminal remedies. In addition, the case managers

3 www.ncmec.org. See appendix for a checklist from the NCMEC.

help identify, develop and promote resources to resolve national and international family abductions through trainings and presentations for the legal and law enforcement communities.

3) If the child has been abducted to or retained in a foreign country, parents also need to contact their local FBI Field Office (http://www.fbi.gov/contact-us/field/listing_by_state) and the U.S. Department of State Office of Children's Issues, (http://www.travel.state.gov/abduction/abduction_580.htm) 1-888-407-4747. Indicators of international child abduction may include packed suitcases and luggage found at the residence, discovery of recently purchased international airline tickets or a recently issued passport for the child and abductor.

In 1980, the United States established the Hague Convention on the Civil Aspects of International Child Abduction, an international treaty that establishes a civil mechanism to ensure the prompt return of children wrongfully removed to or retained outside their country of habitual residence.[4] To use the Hague Convention, parents need to provide evidence of their custodial rights to the child, whether those rights are sole or joint custody rights, and whether they arise by operation of law, court order or legally binding agreement.

Today, there are 100+ countries that are signatory to the Hague Convention. Mexico signed the agreement in 1991. Sadly, the agreement did not grandfather cases prior to that year, so I could not pursue the Hague process for my case. I believe that employing the Hague process would have facilitated aspects of my case.

The U.S. State Department of Children's Issues created a Children's Passport Issuance Alert Program (CPIAP).[5] This program allows parents

---

4 NCMEC

5 U.S. Department of State, http://travel.state.gov/abduction/prevention/passportissuance/passportissuance_554.html

to confirm if a passport has already been issued for their child and receive notification if a passport is requested in the future. Again, in 1987 when Monica and David were abducted, there was no such program in place. Even if there had been, my children did not have passports. All they had were their birth certificates and Carlos had taken those. I did not have copies nor any related documentation.

With few contacts and limited resources at hand, in desperation, I reached out to law enforcement detectives and private investigators. And, even a psychic. I was introduced to Anna, a woman who was a psychic working on cases with law enforcement connected with the Vanished Children's Alliance, a non-profit group dedicated to locating missing and abducted children in the U.S. and abroad (the group ceased operations in 2009). Anna lived in North Carolina and I spoke with her at least six times by phone. Through her intuitive senses, Anna fervently tried to locate where Monica and David might be. While she never pinpointed an exact location, I will never forget that she saw a home with a blue roof in a hilly part of Mexico. There was a white car – an SUV. How incredible it was years later when I learned that the house where Monica and David lived had a blue roof and, yes, Carlos drove a white SUV! I was sad to learn after I found the children that Anna had passed away a few years previously.

Salvador, Investigator in Mexico

I had known Salvador when I worked at an international security company in Mexico City where he was director. It took me about a year to locate him. He was devastated to hear the news about my children and offered to help in any way he could. Salvador only charged expenses for his efforts.

Salvador finally located Carlos and the children in 1989. I could not believe it....I was excited beyond belief! They were living in a town near Toluca about an hour and a half from Mexico City. Salvador learned that Carlos was working for a branch of the state government. Carlos continually changed cars and homes in order to not be discovered. Through neighbors and a nanny who was taking care of Monica and David, Salvador determined that Carlos arranged his schedule to have a tight control over the children's whereabouts. Further, Carlos was to be advised immediately if anyone was looking for him and/or Monica and David.

Salvador and I discussed in-depth if there was any way that we could arrange for me to pick up Monica and David and leave the country safely. Salvador felt there was, but it was not meant to be. Carlos and the children abruptly moved. No one knew where and Salvador, in spite of his efforts, was unable to locate their destination. He was even told that Carlos had left the department of the state government. No one knew where he had gone.

Had Carlos learned about Salvador? Logically, it would appear that he had. I didn't know anyone else in Mexico to call so I tried U.S.-based investigators.

Robert, Private Investigator

I found Robert in the paper. We talked and agreed to meet at a restaurant. I was nervous about the meeting. This was my first introduction to a U.S. private investigator. Robert was a tall, grayish-haired man who wore western attire, including brightly-colored boots. He seemed nice and tried to put me at ease. I am sure he could tell I was uncomfortable.

The more I talked, the easier it became to share about my journey to find Monica and David. Robert seemed to understand and said that he knew individuals who might help him. He assured me that he would do all he could to help me. When I asked him the cost for his services, he said that he would think about and develop a proposed plan.

It was at this point, Robert suggested that we go to a place he knew in the area and have a drink to discuss further. He said that I was attractive and he would like to get to know me better. I immediately declined the invitation and left. Such a program of services Robert was offering!

I'm sad to say that this story isn't so unusual either. There are people who prey on the desperation and neediness of parents for money or other rewards. For example, consider Bill, Richard and Carl…

Bill, Private Investigator

This time I talked with many people through work and personal contacts that provided me with names of people and organizations that helped recover missing children for a fee. One organization, based in North Carolina, gave me Bill's contact information. He was a private investigator and owned a firm. According to his background, Bill was versed in Latin America. He had recovered four children from Argentina and brought them back to the U.S. I spoke with Bill by phone. He seemed credible. I did research about his firm, and it seemed legitimate. Because Bill was based in South Texas and I had to be in San Antonio for business, we agreed to meet at the airport in a café in one of the terminals. The year was 1992. There was no airport security like we have today.

At this time, I was dating Earl who would later become my husband. I asked him to accompany me and observe from a short distance, just in case Bill was another Robert. Bill was a balding man with a huge stomach billowing over his pants. He wore a blue tie and light tan suit jacket and carried a portfolio. He had requested information about Monica and David, including photos. I had everything with me.

I asked a number of questions. Bill provided details about his recovery of the children in Argentina. In my case, his approach would be to first locate Monica and David, determine the schools they were attending and arrange for me then to come to Mexico. We would pick them up and drive to the airport. I would get on a plane and come back to Dallas with my children.

We discussed the cost and he said that the entire operation would cost about $200,000 plus expenses! All I had to do was to give him a down payment of $75,000 to begin his search. I had no such resources.

Calmly, though, I asked him, "How can I guarantee that you will find Monica and David?" Bill quickly assured me that he has been successful before and would be again in locating my children. He had many contacts in Mexico, so it would just be a matter of time.

Bill then excused himself to go to the restroom. Earl later told me that he saw Bill making a phone call. Earl also said that he had seen a tape recorder under the table where Bill and I had been talking.

While Bill was gone, and even before I heard from Earl, I decided I did not trust Bill.

When he returned, I thanked him for his time and said I would give his proposal serious thought and let him know. I never heard from Bill again.

Richard, Private Investigator

I had two other encounters with private investigators. One, Richard, who worked in Las Colinas, also felt that he would be able to find Monica and David and arrange for them to be brought to Texas. His idea was to pick them up, most likely at school, a playground, or a venue away from home. Richard would have a reconstructed Volkswagen. He said he was mechanically savvy with automobiles. I would be in the car, and we would drive to the border. In order not to stop, Richard would have two gas tanks in the car. When we ran out of gas in one, we would use the other. Once we arrived at the border, Monica, David, and I would get out of the car and walk across to Texas. Richard's cost for the entire trip, including the reconstruction of the Volkswagen, was $400,000. All he needed to start was a down payment from me for $100,000.

Carl, Private Investigator

Carl worked for a reputable firm in Dallas or so Earl and I thought. Earl had seen the advertisement for the firm in a suburban newspaper and checked with the Better Business Bureau. Carl met with both of us and stated that he would help find Monica and David. However, he had no experience in arranging for them to be brought back to Dallas.

Carl could not understand why we did not accept his offer to locate the children. He would charge by the hour, approximately $300, once we gave him the green light. Carl kept harassing us with letters for about six months even though we responded that we were not interested.

I wish I could say our experiences were rare or unusual, but I've heard similar stories of shady private investigators from other families. We tried very hard to find reputable practitioners.

Michael, Richardson Police Department

Through David S., I was directed to Michael (Mike) who was a detective for the Richardson Police Department. He also did investigative work on a private basis for a part-time job. He would only charge expenses for any activities he did, which I greatly appreciated.

My attorney in Dallas, Ron, and Mike met and thought that perhaps it would be prudent to make a trip in early 1990 to check the home of Carlos' mother in Mexico City to determine if the children and Carlos might be there. As Ron was trying to coordinate with my Mexican attorney the recognition of the U.S. custody order, he wanted to glean the current whereabouts of Carlos and the children. The only address we had at that time was the mother's address.

Ron and Mike went to Mexico, rented a red Volkswagen, and parked by the mother's condo building. No one was there. Mike even went up to the door and listened. No sounds. Within four hours, Mike and Ron noticed a police car watching them. They left the area with the police following. Fortunately, Ron and Mike were able to get to the airport and left the country without being stopped.

I was nervous while they were gone and could not sleep. As there were no cellphones then, I had no contact with them until they were back in Dallas. When Ron called me to say, "You will not believe what happened!" I froze. When he explained, all I could think of was how lucky they both were to get out of the country. They did not want to go back, and I did not blame them. I also wondered, why choose a **red** Volkswagen? Black, white or tan would have made so much more sense!

Mike was a good guy, but it was still a disappointment. At last Earl and I met John who made all the difference in the world:

John M, Investigator

I met John M through a contact Earl encountered. As I would learn, John worked closely with missing children's organizations. He is gifted in locating missing children. They are his passion, and it hurts him to see children taken from their families, particularly through family abduction. John is a specialist and works exhaustively to find these children. He had located children in Mexico and had various contacts in the country to help him.

The first time I spoke with John in 1998 I knew that we had found the right person at last. After all these years, John was the key to locate Monica and David. I would be reunited with them at last! Through all the winding turns we would take together, all John ever charged was his expenses. He never charged a penny for his time.

Details of John's efforts and ultimate success are detailed later in the book.

Reflections:

- **Do your homework --** I had experiences that would not have been necessary if I had done some investigating of my own ahead of time. Checking with the Better Business Bureau and State Licensing Bureaus is a good start, but it is essential to speak with previous clients about their experiences.

- **Beware of large fees** – A large fee is generally indicative of a scam. If they aren't willing to work with you on a per-hour basis or to have their fee tied to deliverables, then move on. While a modest retainer is reasonable to cover out-of-pocket expenses, $75,000 is not.

- **Look to law enforcement** – Investigators like Mike and John who are referred to you by or by ethical organizations and are driven by a passion to help. They are often more affordable than other practitioners.

- **Avoid magical thinking** – If someone is spinning you a story that sounds too good to be true…it probably is. Tracking down abducted children is hard work with lots of potential dead ends and disappointments along the way. You want confidence and competence in a PI but not promises that can't be kept. You also need to avoid magical thinking. Hiring a PI is not going to solve all your problems and bring your kids back right away. It can take a long time. Things can happen. My first investigator Salvador was planning his extraction when Carlos disappeared again. Set-backs like this are par for the course.

Five

The Waiting Years

At some point it began to sink in that finding the children was going to be a long process. I had to figure out a way to be patient. I needed to find a way to bounce back. I couldn't cry forever. I had to pull myself together. I had to work and support myself. I wrote this chapter to share how I did it. Other parents have done it through other methods. The point is not what you do exactly. It is more about the process of wanting to get back on your feet.

During the first four-to-five years after Monica and David were abducted, I thought of myself as being two people: one person during the day who had a job and interacted with the day to day world, and the other person at night desperately searching for her children. I finally came to realize that I was one and the same person – all aspects of my life contributed to who I was. This being one person in no way diminished my resolve to ever finding Monica and David, but it did help me survive the incredibly long waiting years.

The initial months after Monica and David were abducted were blurs of shock, disbelief, and an overall emotional pit. I would come home from work to an empty house and immediately get on the phone to talk with friends and others who might have ideas. I did not like silence. I had to keep going and be in constant contact with people. All I wanted to do was to determine solutions that would lead me to being with my children again. I was not finding any. I felt so helpless. Then I would cry, and not just cry like in a movie. I kept boxes of Kleenex everywhere in the house. At times, I did not care if I used any tissues. What was the point? No one was there. Who cared what I looked like?

I was depressed. I had trouble sleeping...I experienced more nightmares than I have ever had. Then there were the happy dreams about Monica and David. We would be at the playground, at school, or on the beach playing with toys in the sand. I would wake up and I would think they were there with me. The entire situation was just a bad dream. It was all going to be OK! Then, it would hit me...Monica and David were not there. I was all alone.

Every year I would buy gifts for their birthdays and Christmas. They were an important process and symbol to me, but I never gave them the gifts later after we were reunited. I was mourning my children even though they weren't dead.

I did not want to think about Carlos because when I did all I could feel was anger. He had betrayed me. He had abandoned me and taken the most important people in my life, my heart....my children. He was a villain. And yet, I had been the one who had allowed this to happen. How could I have been so foolish? It was not just a lack of foresight in preventing such an act. I wished I had never met him. Never more would I trust anyone, particularly a man! On and on I would have these internal fights within myself. Feeling guilty, angry, and so, so sad.

At the same time, I knew that I had no way of knowing Carlos would actually abduct Monica and David. No matter how difficult a relationship might be, and even in the midst of a separation or divorce, a parent who abducts his/her children is committing the most extreme and devastating act imaginable for both the children and the other parent.

I had overpowering moments when I wanted to escape into any activity that would make the pain go away. For me, music was my escape, particularly rock and jazz/blues. Sometimes I would sing and dance by myself in the living room. Other times, I sought out a friend and we would go out to listen to music and dance.

I joined a divorce support group at a local church. I wanted to find someone or some group who would understand my situation. In 1988, no such group existed. However, I kept hoping that I would uncover people who had experienced what I was going through.

The support group helped in a way. While I did not find anyone in the group who had been through a similar situation, people empathized and we had camaraderie. Of course, everyone in the group was focused on their own situations and pain. Was it necessary to understand truly what others were going through? I think not. All we wanted to do was to support each other and listen to one another. I had opportunities to talk about how I felt about Carlos and realized that my feelings were normal.

A Realization

One day, I began to look at myself differently. I don't know what happened that caused me to do so. Maybe I realized that it would be longer than I ever imagined finding Monica and David. Maybe I realized I did not like myself and where I was in life. It was time to take stock and look inside. I could not remain in crisis mode forever. I was going to do whatever it took to be OK with me. If I was strong, I would find answers that would lead me to my children. I fervently wanted to be even more as an individual and a mother than prior to the abduction. I wanted to be there in every sense for my children.

I sought counseling. While these professionals did not really grasp what I was experiencing, I developed a renewed sense of confidence. I was determined to build my life and my person. I will never forget one therapist, Anne, with whom I developed a friendship, telling me that the little girl inside me was crying to be loved and appreciated. She had been abandoned by too many people in her life.

Anne was not just referring to Carlos and my children. My own family, parents and sister, were not really there and had abandoned me in many ways throughout my life. I had work to do to overcome obstacles and break through to become someone I really liked.

One key ramification of my experience was and still is the relationship with friends. I had experienced not only parental alienation issues but social alienation.

There have been several loyal and true friends who have supported me throughout my search, recovery and post-recovery stages with Monica and David. While these friends could not relate to what I was experiencing nor understand the situation, they provided unconditional empathy and love.

Other people, even so-called friends, were not supportive and could not understand why I did not just give up hope of ever finding my children. They were critical of my efforts. I let these relationships go.

A big hurdle, particularly in the years when I felt I was two people going through the experience, was dealing with business relationships and with new people I would meet. How much of my personal life should I reveal, particularly when asked the questions: Do you have children? How old are they? Where do they go to school? I decided to simply answer some questions and move on to other topics if I did not feel comfortable in discussing my children.

I have learned throughout the years and to this day that the word normal does not apply to me or my family. Even when children are recovered after being abducted, life does not return to normal. It never will. Rather, it is the new normal. I have also learned that this is OK – people experience life-changing events of various magnitudes and determine their own directions for their lives.

Earl

Earl is a happy part of my new normal. I met him about a year after the abduction in a group therapy support group. We found it was so easy to communicate our feelings even with our respective emotional baggage and challenges. I never thought it would be possible to meet someone who accepted me for who I was without judging my past.

When we started dating, our therapy leader asked us to leave the group (no dating allowed!).We married in July, 1992, five years after Monica and David had been abducted. Earl is my true advocate and inspiration. He made the commitment to be there in the search for Monica and David and has played an integral parenting role since we found them. With his patience and level headedness, he has helped keep me on track when I have gone through frustration, periods of hopelessness and fear. We have cried together, celebrated together, sparred together, and been there for each other. We have built a life together. We enjoy activities together and exploring new experiences. We love to travel, eat in unusual restaurants, go to music festivals, and play tennis on occasion. Earl has an antique business, so we often explore towns and go shopping.

Reflections from Earl:

Being kicked out of the support group brought us even closer together. Until Susan got her children back, however, it seemed like the relationship would not get serious. One day I told her that I was in it for the duration. At the time, I don't know if I meant until the children were back or for the duration of our lives, but it turns out I meant the latter.

Initially, we thought we would get the children back at any time and we wanted to wait to get married. In 1992, we decided not to keep our lives on hold for any longer. Susan is the rose of my life and I'm so happy we married when we did.

Sometimes Susan would get very depressed over the loss of Monica and David. She would get crazy ideas born out of desperation and frustration that we would try to do until she realized it wouldn't work. For example, she got the idea to disguise ourselves and go to Mexico and try and find Monica and David. We went to a costume shop and bought wigs, accessories and clothes to make ourselves look Mexican. If we had tried to use these ridiculous costumes, we would have found ourselves probably in jail and would not have seen the light of day for a long time. We still laugh today about that crazy plan.

Career Moves

The accounting software company for which I worked at the time of the abduction became a stepping stone for my professional career. Ever so fortunately, in spite of the emotional and physical turmoil I was undergoing, I did not lose my job. I will never forget my boss, Kevin, saying that he had full confidence that I would continue being effective in my position in the midst of crisis. He felt I could manage both – even at times when I needed to miss work due to activities related to my search for Monica and David.

I remained at the company until 1994, leaving as director of corporate communications. In addition to my work activities, prior to leaving the company, I became accredited in public relations with the Public Relations Society of America (PRSA). I became very active in PRSA both locally and regionally, where I was president of the local chapter one year and served as a district chair for the southwest region. I attended various national and regional conventions and really enjoyed the activities and meeting wonderful and talented people. I also had opportunities to speak at various conferences on PR related topics. I became involved with local community organizations, American Heart Association's Women Heart Health and Junior Achievement-North Texas chapter and participated in board of director activities.

In 1994, with Earl's encouragement, I started my own public relations firm. Experiencing the highs and lows of a small business owner, I achieved success in managing communications activities for emerging and large companies, primarily in technology. When the technology bubble burst at the end of the 90's, I began to migrate into other industries, like transportation, energy, and real estate. Even though my firm has seen two to three metamorphoses, including a downsizing of staff and challenges with business partners, I feel proud of what I have accomplished. Most of all, I feel confident in my abilities and expertise that continue to grow. I truly love my profession!

Faith and Trust

Prior to the abduction, I had questioned the existence of God. The abduction changed me spiritually. Today I believe that not only does God exist, but that I have been guided all the way through the search and recovery of my children. There was and is a timeline that only God knows. At so many steps along the way, God has been with me.

Further, Earl and I deeply feel that God brought us together to help find Monica and David and become a family. We have learned to trust and truly love, feelings that I seriously doubted were possible when the abduction occurred.

After Earl and I married, we joined a neighborhood Presbyterian Church. We became active; I joined the choir, which I enjoyed. I re-discovered a love I had always had for singing. I even sang a few solos and took voice lessons. I felt so at peace when I sang. This was true therapy in ways a professional would find difficult to replicate.

Step-by-step I created a life for myself that was more than my rage towards Carlos and my grief over Monica and David. I call these the growing years for me because I grew up. I became a better person than I was before. Earl was a huge part of my recovery because he helped me trust and because family was so important to him.

Six

Found!

In the spring of 1998, Earl connected with a contact that referred us to John, an investigator who worked closely with law enforcement and organizations that focused on recovering children who were missing. John's passion was to locate such children and he dealt with difficult cases.

As mentioned earlier, when Earl and I spoke with John, he felt so strongly about our search that he agreed to do whatever he could to locate them. Knowing the extraordinary amount of money that I had spent over the years, John agreed to take the case and only charge expenses. His one request was for me to compile a binder or booklet with all documentation, photos, information about Carlos and his family, last known addresses, etc. I made several copies so that he could distribute them.

John had investigator friends with whom he worked in Mexico on missing children cases. Using knowledge and means known to them, they uncovered a few potential locations where Carlos and the children might be. These leads proved to be dead ends, yet the investigators thought Carlos and the children were in the general geographic area.

One of the Mexican investigators connected us to a family law attorney in Mexico City, Jose Luis.

Jose Luis agreed to help John and the other investigators search for Monica and David and only charge expenses for his efforts. Earl and I were so overwhelmed by his generosity and so hopeful that this time might be different. Jose Luis requested a video about my search for my children – he believed this would be valuable once they were located.

Being in the public relations industry, locating someone who would do the video was not difficult. What was important was to find the right firm or individual who had compassion and empathy for the situation. After visiting with several, I found the perfect team, Terry, who attended our church with his wife and business partner, Liza. Terry staged the video in our home. He wanted the video to be homey, loving, and simple.

Once again I felt God's influence on the venture. The video was Terry and Liza's gift to me. Their only goal was that the video would help in locating and reuniting me with Monica and David.

Terry wanted me to tell my story. He had me sit on the sofa holding my cat, Sari, with Monica and David's toys surrounding my feet. I talked to the camera and shared how much I loved and missed them. I talked about Sari and asked Monica if she remembered what a sweet and loving cat she was. We did a number of takes – I have no idea how many. I choked up and cried often. I was drained when we had finished.

When Earl and I saw the final version of the video, Terry had captured the heart and all the feelings from the years I had been searching. I was pleased with the results. My stomach, though, was in knots. Would Monica and David ever see it?

Spring 1999

Jose Luis believed he had found Monica's school in Toluca. His plan was to have one of his female attorneys, Lupita, take the video to Monica and to have a conversation with her. I didn't know what day she would go. It was a terribly long week and it was hard to work. By Friday, I assumed it would be another week before I heard anything. It was so hard to be patient!

Lupita was concerned that the conversation with Monica would not actually happen. She feared she would be blocked by the director or other school officials from visiting Monica between classes or during her lunch break. We prayed hard.

When Lupita called on April 2, I was over the moon with joy. Excitedly, I asked Lupita to describe Monica. She said that Monica was pretty and very slender with big brown eyes and a sweet smile. Monica conveyed intelligence, Lupita said, even with the few words she spoke during their conversation.

My daughter was a young woman! I was so thrilled to have found her at last. Lupita had given her the video, a phone card to call me, and her business card. Now we had to wait for her to watch it. I wanted to fly to Mexico immediately, but there was more to do first.

The Next Phone Call

I did not actually meet Monica and David until the first weekend in September. First I had a series of phone conversations with both children. Jose Luis suggested delaying the reunion for several months. It was imperative to be cautious and take one step at a time. Jose Luis first had to convince Carlos to accept the re-opening of communication between Monica, David, and me. Not surprisingly, Carlos was resistant.

Now that there were lawyers involved and the international laws were changing, Carlos' position of power had been diminished. I now had legal leverage, and the children were pressuring him to talk to me. Our first phone conversation was arranged for Saturday, April 17 at 2:00 p.m. with Carlos initiating the call. While I did not like the idea of Carlos being involved in the call, there was nothing I could do to stop it.

I was nervous to say the least. Would the call happen or would Carlos play games with me again? What would be my first words to

Monica and David? How would I react to the sound of Carlos' voice? I shared these feelings with Earl and as always, he understood the depth of my uncertainty of what was about to take place.

I had growing feelings of trepidation and insecurity. I knew that I would be hearing Monica's and David's voices for the first time in so many years. How would they sound? Would Monica have the same voice as she did when she was five? Of course not, I told myself. She was now almost 18. Except for a "goo goo ga" and a faintly distinctive "mama," I did not know what David's voice even sounded like. Now 15, would his voice be strong, soft, or loud? Would this?.....Would that?........So many questions kept churning through my mind.

After all my worries, the first call was calm, oddly superficial and formal. It was like we were in a class and asked to describe our summer vacation or a recent trip. In this case, the vacation or trip spanned a period of twelve years!

When I hung up the phone from that first telephone conversation, I felt the hesitancy, the lack of trust, and sadness that underscored everything that had been said by the children and me. Were these feelings due to Carlos being on the phone? Probably, to some extent. However, I believe it was more due to us being strangers. Monica, David, and I were related but we did not know one another.

As subsequent phone conversations would prove, there were no visible changes in terms of communication between the children and me. We might have begun to feel more comfortable talking with each other, but there were still no outward signs of emotional or topical depth. Monica and David talked about their school activities and what they had been doing with their friends. I talked about what I had been doing and what was happening in Dallas and the U.S. in general. That was all the three of us could discuss at this juncture in our relationship.

Although the telephone conversations provided me some insight into Monica and David's everyday lives, I knew that I would not understand who they really were until I saw them in person. This would be the true heart reunion for which I had been longing and dreaming for years.

Labor Day Weekend 1999

The anticipation for our first meeting was excruciating. New passports had been received and plane tickets had been purchased. Arrangements had been made to stop the mail, have someone feed our cats, and to board our pug, Crumpet. Our suitcases were packed, including an extra bag of gifts for Monica and David. A couple from church had offered to pick us up the next morning and take us to the airport. I had time on my hands and I fidgeted while my mind raced and my heart pounded.

Earl and I did not know what to expect. Although I had spoken with both of them almost every week since our first phone conversation in April, I was scared, excited, and nervous. This would be the first time I would actually see and possibly hug and kiss Monica and David for twelve years. This reunion would make everything real. Earl was worried about my safety and well-being since he would not be there at the reunion.

Jose Luis, our attorney in Mexico, had meticulously planned our visit and reunion. We would stay in Mexico for four days. His driver, Pedro, would meet Earl and me at the airport and take us to Jose Luis' home where we would stay during our trip. The following evening, Pedro and I would go to Toluca for the reunion with Monica and David. Earl would remain behind at Jose Luis' home. Jose Luis believed in taking precautions. He was concerned about Carlos' behavior when the actual meeting occurred. Further, Jose Luis knew that Carlos had contacts in the government who might prove to be adversarial towards us.

This time we made sure many people knew our itinerary including our families and friends. Our minister Roger even shared our story with the church. Many members called us or sent cards with their support and prayers before we left. We were overwhelmed with gratitude. God was blessing us over and over again.

Everything went as planned. On the day of the reunion, Jose Luis reconfirmed with Carlos that he would bring Monica and David at 7:00 p.m. to the Quinta Del Rey, a small hotel in Toluca, where we would meet at the restaurant entrance.

I kept trying to decide what to wear and was concerned how my hair and makeup looked. I wanted to be me. I hoped Monica and David would be proud of their mom. I wanted to demonstrate I was healthy, strong, and confident. I finally decided on a colorful red and orange jacket, red and black shoes, and black pants. I wore a red scarf, gold earrings, a long gold necklace, and black/gold bracelet. It was much more nerve-wracking than any date I had ever been on before.

Although I had brought gifts with me, I decided not to take them for our first visit. I did not know what to expect and did not want the gifts to be the primary focus. I did not want to act like I was showering my children with material items to gain their affection and acceptance.

I brought with me photos of Monica and David when they were small, photos of the house where I lived, the cats, Sari and Oreo, and our dog Crumpet. Toluca is about two hours west of downtown Mexico City. Due to the city's horrendous traffic, the trip often takes much longer. From Coyocan where Jose Luis lives, the drive is typically two and half hours. Since it was a Friday, we left three hours early.

Pedro and I chatted amiably in Spanish and I learned that he had worked for Jose Luis for a number of years. He served as Jose Luis' driver, messenger, and on occasion, a bodyguard. He didn't say so, but I realized that there was a gun underneath that black leather jacket. Suddenly the trip seemed like a TV or movie crime thriller. It was unreal.

We arrived at the Quinta Del Rey Hotel about 6:30 and Pedro said that I was not to worry; he would be watching me every minute. He contacted Jose Luis and let him and Earl know that we were at the hotel. Then he went to find an observation spot.

Waiting, Waiting, Waiting

About 7:10 p.m., I could not sit any longer. I started walking around the restaurant. I began to wonder if Monica and David would show up. Would Carlos decide at the last minute not to bring them? The minutes dragged by slowly.

At about 8:15, I spoke with Pedro who suggested that we continue to wait for at least another 45 minutes.

When still they had not arrived by 9:15, I decided to leave. The children were not going to come. Carlos' promise to Jose Luis was a farce and a lie…again.

I could not find Pedro right away; however. When I spotted him a few minutes later, he nodded his head and motioned for me to turn around. Walking towards the restaurant from the hotel lobby were two teenagers, Carlos, and a woman who was holding his hand.

Reunion

I stood transfixed. After all the walking and pacing I had done while waiting, now I could not move.

The four walked up to me. I could not believe it…..Monica and David were no longer babies! They looked so grown up! Monica was now 18; David 15.

Carlos said hello and introduced the woman as his wife. Her name was Rosa. They each wore wedding bands although I learned later they were not married. She was a rent-a-wife for lack of a better description. Carlos never gave any reason why they were so late. His words were slurred. I suspected he had been drinking.

I just kept looking at Monica and David. Monica and David stepped forward. We didn't hug. Their expressions were cold and withdrawn.

The three of us had dinner, although none of us were able to eat much. Carlos and Rosa were seated nearby. Up to this point, we had hardly said three words among us. We were silent except for ordering our meals. Suddenly, Monica looked at me darkly and said, "I thought you were dead!" Almost immediately, David turned to me and asked, "If you knew where we were, why didn't you come sooner to see us? Why now?"

I was taken back, yet not surprised. I began to share all that had happened during the years since they had been taken and how I did not know where they were. I was careful not to use the word abducted. Something told me both children would react angrily and shut the door for further conversation. I did not talk negatively about their father. My words were confined to my activities: My starting a PR firm; how much I like sports, reading, and music. Most importantly, I wanted Monica and David to know how I had finally found them, how much I had missed and loved them, and how much I wanted to get to know them.

Now I wanted to know all about them. I was anxious to hear about their lives. How was school? What subjects did they like? Their teachers, their friends. What sports and activities did they like? Monica and David talked generally. Monica liked science, astronomy, and literature. David liked history and sports, particularly soccer. He did not like math. Monica talked about starting college at the Technological Universidad de Monterrey, Toluca campus. She was planning to study business marketing.

I could see the hurt in their eyes. They seemed so confused and angry. They said that they were not sure we would ever be friends, let alone anything more.

At 11:00 p.m., we got up to leave. We still didn't hug.

We agreed to meet the following day at the shopping mall in Toluca.

Pedro was waiting for me outside the door to the parking lot. I shared with him what had happened. For most of the trip back to Jose Luis', though, I was silent.

Saturday morning I awoke still living the surreal dream of the previous night's visit. My feelings were a blur of love, disappointment, confusion, anger, and most of all, deep sadness. Nothing had been magically resolved by seeing each other. My children and I were strangers. It was so hard for me to grasp this, let alone accept that they were ambivalent – at best – about meeting me.

Although I had tried not to set high expectations of this first face-to-face visit with Monica and David, I had hoped that after the phone conversations we had had, the visit would be different. While logically I knew that patience would have to overrule the frustrations if I wanted to develop a long-term relationship with my children, emotionally was another story.

After acknowledging my disappointment and overly optimistic expectations, I pulled myself together and began to get ready for our second visit. I gathered the clothing items I had for each, glad again that I had not taken these with me for the first visit. Earl gave me a particularly strong hug before I left with Pedro.

The weather that day in Toluca was cloudy and cool with showers. We arrived in the parking lot of the mall near the designated entrance and agreed this time to meet there at 1 p.m. I was not sure if Monica and David would want to visit with me for three hours or if I would feel equally uncomfortable with them. However, I thought that with eating lunch, the time would be just right for this visit.

I took my gift bags into the mall and waited by the benches where we had agreed to meet. This time, Monica and David arrived close to 1 p.m. Carlos was with them as well as Monica's boyfriend Caesar. Once again, I wondered how I could possibly even begin to connect with my children with their father hovering closely by.

I was determined to have a pleasant visit. Monica, David, and I went over to a bench where I gave them their clothing gifts. They were polite but I could tell that they really did not care for my selections. Of course, I understood my mistake immediately. I had purchased what I thought they would like and wear without knowing who they really were and what their tastes would be.

Next, we started walking the mall in a group. Monica walked with Caesar, David with his father, and I was somewhere in between. I definitely did not belong, yet everyone tried to maintain appearances. I conversed with Monica and Caesar, a nice young man who was enraptured with Monica. David and I talked some. He appeared to be in forced conversation with his father, and he separated himself when he could. However, whether I conversed with David or Monica, the topics were superficial and non-threatening. Masked conversation seemed more comfortable.

We walked most of the mall and checked out different stores. David asked Monica several times if she liked a certain item he wanted to buy. He wanted her approval. She responded with combined motherly and sisterly comments. In my absence, Monica was David's mother role model. My heart ached tremendously. I thought how sad and difficult it had been all these years for both of them without me.

Conversation slowed considerably at lunch. Carlos' presence was unnerving. I could not believe that I was sitting near the man who had stolen my children from me! His deceit and inexcusable actions the previous night made the situation even more reprehensible.

Yet, I kept it to myself. I knew that if I were ever to have a relationship with Monica and David, I would need to interact with and tolerate their father at some level. I had to determine the level that would be tolerable for me. As I have shared with parents whose children have been abducted and recovered, the focus must be on their children and not feelings against the abducting parents. This focus is incredibly important in order to build relationships with our children. In most cases, they love their other parent and are protective of them.

It was getting close to 4:00 p.m. and time leave. Carlos asked who was picking me up. I said I had a driver. His interest was suspicious.

As we walked towards the door, I arranged to meet Monica and David the following morning at a restaurant on the square. I started to hug them, but then decided it best to refrain. Caesar took a photo of the three of us. When I look at it today, the expressions on each of our faces are so telling. The sadness, the yearning, and anger shout from the smiles.

Since it was Saturday, the mall was busy, so it took several minutes for us to leave the parking lot. Pedro kept looking at the rearview mirror and I asked him why. He said that he was watching Carlos' white SUV. How did Pedro know this? He had seen it when he had checked out where Carlos and the children were living. Carlos also had another vehicle which he had used the night before.

Now, I began to look in the rearview mirror as the white SUV followed us. When we left the parking lot, Pedro went down a street that was different from the one we had driven earlier in the day. The white SUV followed us.

Pedro took evasive maneuvers. He sped through small neighborhoods and towns with narrow streets. Some were unpaved. Others were cobblestone. There were vendors on almost every corner selling juices, soft drinks, tacos, and corn on the cob, all very typical of small, poor locales in Mexico. Pedro's driving was incredible. He maneuvered over pot holes and rugged pavement without hitting anyone during his tight turns. He lost the white SUV.

I had no idea where we were except that I knew we were not anywhere close to the highway between Toluca and Mexico City, and that the white SUV was no longer behind us. I glanced at my watch. It was 6 p.m., two hours since we had left the mall.

When we finally reached the highway, I thanked Pedro for the scenic tour.

When we arrived at Jose Luis' house at 8:00 p.m., the look on Earl's face spoke volumes. This had been one of the longest days he had ever experienced. He had spent most of the afternoon walking up and down the driveway, worried.

Jose Luis was particularly concerned when I described the white SUV following us. He, more than anyone, understood the ramifications.

Moreover, he was cognizant of Carlos' position and his connections with the state of Mexico's government. This authority was especially powerful and corrupt in the country.

That night at dinner I drank too much and got a terrible headache. We went to bed early where I promptly collapsed and went to sleep.

The next morning, Earl and I got ready to leave with Pedro for Toluca and then the airport. This time Earl would be there if something happened.

When Pedro pulled out of Jose Luis' driveway, I noticed a white car parked outside. Earl noticed that there was a man slumped down in the seat. We didn't know what to think. Later, we learned that a member of our church was a retiree from the CIA and he had contacted and made arrangements with someone to "keep an eye on us." At the time, it was unnerving. Yesterday was a car chase. What would happen today?

When we arrived in Toluca, Pedro parked in an underground parking garage near the square. Earl remained in the car. Monica and David arrived at the restaurant on time. Their father was with them. Monica wanted him to eat with us. I did not say a word. None of us spoke very much during the meal. What a family scene…..if only others in the restaurant knew the story!

After brunch, I told Carlos I wanted to visit with Monica and David before I had to leave for the airport. Carlos left.

We walked to the square and looked at the statues and gardens. They told me about the history of Toluca and about its culture, and what the people were like today. We took photos. We kept the conversation light and general. I wanted to say more, but I could not bring myself to do it. I struggled to find the words to say.

It was time to leave. I dreaded saying goodbye. My eyes filled up. I planned to return in a few months. In the meantime, I suggested that we talk every Sunday evening. Would they like that? They half-heartedly said OK. This time I gave each one a hug. They did not reject me, but their hugs were perfunctory. After all this time, I wanted to hold on. It was so hard to let go.

It was a tough visit but an important beginning. The job of building our family from scratch seemed so daunting, but I wanted it more than anything in the world.

Reflections from Earl:

I was about to become a stepparent of older children. I had no idea what on earth I had gotten myself into, but I quickly learned that patience and prayer were required. When Pedro took off with Susan to the town of Toluca to meet Monica and David for dinner, I thought that was the longest afternoon and evening that I have ever spent in my life. The attorney's home is placed on a large lot about the length of two football fields inside a block fence that goes around his compound. I must have paced for hours.

The next day at the mall was even worse because she was supposed to be home much earlier. I was afraid something had happened.

The driver took us to Toluca for Susan to meet Monica and David for lunch. He parked in a dark, very dirty underground parking garage and left me there inside the car for hours until Susan got back. The only people I saw were a couple of guys with buckets of water washing cars. That first trip was very hard and I was glad to get home.

Seven

The Building Years

After that first visit, we arranged more trips and made weekly phone calls. About a year later, Carlos lost his job with the state government in Toluca. A new president and party had assumed leadership of Mexico and his job was eliminated.

Carlos moved to Cuernavaca to be near his brother, Ramon, who said that he would help him locate a position in a state or local governmental office. Monica was attending college at Tec de Monterrey in Toluca. Since she and David were moving too, Monica needed to transfer to the campus in Cuernavaca.

There was one obstacle. Carlos was strapped financially, so he could no longer afford to send Monica to college. Although she had received a partial scholastic scholarship to college, she was still responsible to pay the balance of the fees and class materials. David was in a quandary since the public schools in Cuernavaca were poor academically.

Earl and I decided to help both children financially with their education. Had we not helped them, neither Monica nor David would have graduated from college. We explored the options of them moving to the

U.S. and going to high school/college here. Neither Monica nor David was ready at that point to make such a move.

And so began a new journey for the four of us. Monica transferred to Tec de Monterrey – University in Cuernavaca and David enrolled in the high school/preparatory of Tec de Monterrey. Both children blossomed in their new schools. We knew we had made the right decision to help even though it was difficult for us financially. I established a good relationship with the school which helped us with payment schedules and other matters.

We were so proud when both Monica and David graduated! Monica came up to me after her ceremony and said, "I would never have graduated without you and your help." She was crying and so was I. Days like this were what I had dreamed about during the long years we were separated.

Monica received a job offer from a large company, Unilever, while we were there for the graduation, and she was so proud of herself. Even though it was in Mexico City, she was ecstatic. Her hard work and dedication to her studies during college had paid off.

David was selected as the most social of his class. He celebrated by wearing a white suit and dancing the night away at his graduation party while girls stood in line. He looked so happy, actually one of the happiest times I have seen him. David was on top of the world. I treasure the moment when he told me how proud he was for me to be there celebrating with him.

Our visits with Monica and David changed during the time they were both in school. Our trips to Mexico were more frequent. Both Monica and David seemed to enjoy spending more time with me and then us. They met Earl for the first time on an early visit to Cuernavaca. Monica, David and I were having lunch at the Las Mananitas Hotel. Earl was taking a walk nearby when David recognized him from photos. It was natural for me to bring Earl over and make introductions. The informality of their meeting, along with Earl's patience, helped their relationship evolve comfortably with him. There was no pressure because Earl knew to take it step-by-step.

We had relaxing and fun times together. Earl and I found a driver who picked us up at the airport every time we went to Mexico. Octavio helped to foster relationships in town for us.

Yet there was always a cloud in the shape of Carlos. Monica and David did not talk much about him and avoided serious conversations about the past. According to Monica and David, Carlos had to make frequent mandatory visits to Toluca. They said it was because the government owed him money and there had been a problem. Earl and I speculated with each other that he was on probation or conducting community service. What we noticed over the years is that after losing his job in Toluca, except for brief stints of work with one of his brothers, he never obtained another position in any governmental agency or corporation.

Monica and David wanted to live in the present and move forward. In many ways so did we. We were focused on having a relationship first and left it to them to ask questions when they were ready.

Living with Monica

When Monica was a junior in college, she had the opportunity to participate in a student exchange program to spend a semester at a college/university in another country. Two of the colleges were Southern Methodist University (SMU) in Dallas and Rice University, Houston, Texas. Monica researched the various opportunities in different cities and countries and approached me about coming to Texas to attend one of the colleges here. Her reason was loud and clear. She wanted to have the opportunity to get to know me and Earl better.

I was ecstatic! I excitedly researched both school programs and talked with various representatives. After helping Monica with the application process and doing the necessary financial paperwork, she was accepted to SMU. In August 2003, Monica arrived in the U.S. and Dallas for the first time since being abducted.

I had so much fun getting her room and bathroom ready! I felt like an expectant mother. Earl and I found furniture for the room, including a desk. We bought a TV and had a phone installed. I spent hours looking for linens and accessories. The day she arrived there were beautiful flowers on her desk with a welcome poster. We told friends that Monica was coming to spend the semester with us. They could not wait to meet her. One of my closest friends planned a visit to Dallas from Washington State when she heard the news.

The first few months after Monica arrived were spent in getting settled and adapting both to school and to us as a family. Monica worked hard. Her coursework was difficult, so she had to spend many hours studying. Earl or I would take her to school, pick her up, and generally accompany her on errands as needed. She got her driver's license and was happy to be independent. She missed her father and brother and called them once a week.

I later learned that one of the hurdles Monica encountered was not being accepted by other students at school. SMU was a culture shock. There was an attitude towards Mexico that she did not understand. I wanted so much for Monica to feel accepted by our friends and community that I sometimes forced situations. There were people at church who were ill at ease when they spoke with us. "A beautiful girl," many would say. However, they kept a certain distance and didn't introduce Monica to their families. Our eyes were opened to prejudice at our church and we had to find another church.

One night at dinner, Monica, Earl, and I had a conversation that led to me saying how wonderful it was to have Monica with us after so many years. Earl commented that she would one day perhaps understand all the efforts that the both of us had undergone to find and reunite with her and David after the abduction.

When Earl said the word abduction and mentioned her father, Monica jumped up from the table and ran to her room upset like I had never seen her. When I went to her room, she talked about Earl. He did not have the right to talk about her father. Earl did not know him and all that he had done for both her and David. Besides that, Monica vehemently declared, Earl did not have the same intellectual capability that I did in understanding the situation. Obviously, Monica felt very protective of her father.

Her reaction is common in familial abductions. She doesn't see herself as kidnapped because she was with her dad. She glosses over the fact that he took her away from me, lied to her about me and did everything he could not to be found. That his actions are a crime punishable by a jail sentence in the U.S. is also beyond her comprehension. He is her dad and she loves him. It is more important to have a relationship with Monica than for her to see the truth about her dad. One day she will want to look at the situation more closely and I'll be there for her.

After that evening, the relationship between the three of us was strained although polite. A hole was growing in the pit of my stomach when I realized the semester would soon end. How I wished Monica would consider staying and completing her studies at SMU! I did not want to lose her again.

I arranged a trip to visit my mother in Hendersonville, North Carolina so that Monica would have an opportunity to see her again. We took a road trip through Atlanta. I showed her where I used to live and go to high school and college. I hoped that being on a road trip of just Monica and me would open doors for our relationship. We had fun and this was the beginning of our mother – daughter weekends that we enjoy today.

My mother did not want us to stay with her and expressed the wish that we could visit at another time. While uncomfortable, these challenges opened the door for Monica and me to talk about family, including my sister, Cheryl. I know my mother was happy to see Monica despite her issues. Monica was grateful to see her grandmother and begin to meet that side of her family. Sadly, this was the last time they saw each other. Mom passed away three years later. I remember watching

Monica walking around her dining and living rooms looking at photos and absorbing the people to whom she was related. This was family too, I achingly felt.

After this trip, I had to go to Philadelphia for a client. I asked Monica if she would like to go and she jumped at the chance to accompany me. Once again, it was a fun trip. I was happy and I think Monica was too. Memories were being made.

Monica enjoyed our yearly sojourn to Mo Ranch during Thanksgiving. She appreciated the time and the peace. She seemed to relax with us and friends with whom we connect each year. Bringing her into our traditions helped her feel part of our family.

With December drawing near and the conclusion of the semester, Monica was focused on completing projects and studying for final exams. I dreaded that the end of the year was quickly approaching when Monica would leave. Her heart was definitely not here in Dallas. She wanted to go back to Mexico to be with her father, brother and a guy in her class with whom she had begun to fall in love. I was going to lose her and I felt sad.

The day after Christmas, I received a call from my best friend's husband. Carolyn had suffered a heart attack the previous night and died. I was devastated. Carolyn was only 51 years old – too young to depart this world. The next several days were a shock and blur while I helped her husband and family make funeral preparations. I cried frequently. Monica felt my grief and was at my side although she still left as scheduled for Mexico. If it happened today, I know she would stay, but at that moment, I had not only lost one of my best friends, I felt I was losing my daughter once again.

When Earl and I took her to the airport, I cried like I never had. Monica was shaken too; however, she seemed relieved to be leaving. I was sad but determined that no matter what had happened or would in the future, we would see each other again to continue our relationship journey.

Living with David

I used to receive frequent texts from David asking if I would "lend" him money to pay his cell phone bill. How many similar texts about money have I received from my now 26-year-old son? I have begun to lose count. The message was always the same: "Mom, would you lend me XX amount to pay XX? As soon as I have a job, I will pay you back." There were a number of times during the last several years when I would lend him the cash. However, for the past few years, my answer is, "No."

The abduction affected David profoundly, more so than Monica in many ways. Being only a year and a half when he was abducted, David had not yet attached with me. He grew up relying on Monica to be his mother. I was not part of his important developmental years but finally appeared halfway through his adolescence. We were strangers. I suspect that at a subconscious level, we both understood why. We are survivors yet polarized in how we approach survival.

As any parent knows, children are different. They inherit some characteristics from their mothers and others from their fathers to develop their own distinctive identities. I discovered after getting to know David that he has traits that parallel my own. He is social, sensitive, adventurous and creative. He is quick to lend a hand to anyone in trouble and trusts what people say. As I had to learn, David is realizing that he cannot always trust everyone or what they say. He has to recognize and discern what is true or not. At the same time, his ability to focus and complete one task at a time is a challenge for him just like it was for me until I was well into adulthood. The dreamer part of being an Aquarian definitely is a factor here.

David is complex. There was a disturbing and sometimes dark side to him during this period. He had a Dr. Jekyll, Mr. Hyde persona. David had no fundamental drive and ambition to succeed on his own. He believed that there is always someone who will help him. At times, he would be deceitful to get what he wants. For several years, I thought that David was exhibiting the immaturity of youth. I suspect now there was something deeper in his fabric that may always exist or perhaps disappear with years.

After David graduated from high school at Tecnologico (Tec) de Monterrey, he wanted to pursue business administration in college. Earl and I agreed to pay his tuition.

Tec is a tough school, and David struggled almost from the start. He felt comfortable with the students and professors but erratic in his classes. Exams, in particular, were difficult for him. He was always nervous. With the subjects he found challenging, it was especially painful. When he was "on" in a subject, his grades were off the charts. When he was off on a subject, his grades sank. David kept promising he would do better; however, the unpredictability continued. He failed a few classes, received A's in others.

About two years after David started college and following a particularly difficult semester, he wanted to talk with Earl and me. He was excited to share an idea that he had. Knowing that we would soon be coming to Mexico for a visit, David agreed to wait until we were there so that he could tell us in person.

One evening, Earl, Monica, David and I gathered in a hotel dining room where David had a PowerPoint presentation on his computer. Like a business meeting, David had spent hours compiling the content. We were proud of his efforts.

David had begun to question whether college was for him. He thought that there may be another direction he should take. He visited with his best friend, Carlos, who was an airline pilot, and said that he became fascinated with the idea of flying. With Carlos, David visited several aviation schools in Mexico City. In his presentation, he outlined detailed descriptions for each. David was quick to point out that compared to college fees, the costs involved with these schools were considerably less. David also felt that the time involved to complete training at an aviation school was shorter than obtaining a college degree.

We all discussed David's option at length. Earl and I agreed to explore David's interest in attending aviation school and we scouted out the top two schools from his list during our visit. We ultimately agreed on one school, Pratt Aviation, and reconfirmed with David his desire to become a pilot.

David liked his classroom instruction. He performed admirably. Although the content was hard, David seemed focused. He wanted to pass his coursework so that he could begin his practicum of actual flying. We were so pleased for him. It was also at this time that David became very interested in a woman he had met during high school at Tec, and they started dating. Her name was Diana.

I had originally met Diana and her mother at David's graduation from high school. At that time, she was planning to pursue a degree in engineering at Tec. Both she and her mother seemed very nice and gracious. Little did I dream what my next encounter with Diana's mother would entail.

David started falling in love with Diana at his high school graduation party. Over time he had developed a good relationship with Diana's family. At times, he said, the parents treated him like their own son. All of this sounded great, but we were not prepared for how obsessed he became with her later.

In the spring of 2010, David was ready to initiate the practical aspect of aviation. In order to earn his private flying license, he had to dedicate a guaranteed number of hours to pilot instruction and practice. The Pratt school had two locations for students to train: Cuernavaca and McAllen, Texas. David opted to do his in McAllen.

Per Pratt's policy, the students had housing at a Holiday Inn Extended Stay hotel near the airport. David and three other young men shared a two-bedroom suite. Each shared the expenses. Although the families helped their respective sons, some parents, including us, encouraged them to find employment to defray their expenses. The students had available time since their actual instruction classes consumed only several hours a week.

Jobs were scarce in McAllen, or at least that is what David said. At the same time, David was trying to improve his English and took classes twice a week to help him. However, he quickly grew bored because they were not sufficiently conversational.

After a month and a half, David began to be frustrated with the limited flying time that was provided to him and the other students. There were a minimal number of planes and licensed pilots to train the students. Weather, always a factor, presented additional barriers to actual flight time. David was impatient. He was anxious to complete his practical instruction and obtain his private license. Earl and I encouraged him to keep his spirits up.

We also decided that it would be valuable to check with other aviation schools in the U.S. to determine if they had similar formats for actual flying instruction. Our path led us to American Flyers, a nationwide school with a facility in Dallas. They allow students to fly every day and there is always a pilot available to teach.

We discussed American Flyers at length with David and arranged for a preliminary interview. He was accepted. We happily cleaned and prepared David's room so he could live with us. We made travel reservations for David. We bought extra food and other necessities. Earl and I did everything to prepare for David's arrival. Except for one thing...... the most important item of all. WE were not prepared. Neither was David.

Earl and I had not given enough thought about our roles while David lived with us. How would we feel having our son, a young adult, be part of our everyday activities? It had been more than five years since Monica had lived with us. Although we had had a few rough moments, overall the experience had been positive. Incredibly so. Our bonding, individually and collectively, began during this time. Why would we NOT have the same experience with David?

He arrived in June and we were so excited. He was focused on getting his private flying license, so he concentrated on studying and flying when he was scheduled. Life became a routine for all of us. I was working hard; Earl was working. We seemed to all be jelling naturally.

David obtained his private flying license at the end of July. He wanted to go on a vacation to South Padre Island with his friends from the school in McAllen to celebrate obtaining his license. Our only advice to him was that he and his friends should not cross into Mexico due to recent border town violence. He agreed.

Friday night I received a call from David saying that his friend's car had broken down (flat tire), so he was unable to get back to McAllen in time to catch the bus for Dallas. I asked him where he was. When he said between Monterrey and Reynoso, I got upset and asked him why they were in Mexico? Hadn't he said that he would not go to Mexico? After a crazy story about why the visit to South Padre had not worked out and that he and his friends had decided to go to Monterrey to see some friends, all I could say was for him to come back to Dallas. We talked about his trip to Mexico when David came home. He apologized and said that he did not know what to do since the friend had been driving and David had no other means of transportation.

This episode began a series of bizarre episodes with David fabricating stories so that he could do what he wanted to do. We learned that what he wanted to do was to be with Diana; his focus was only on her. He talked about pursuing a commercial pilot's license; that was his ultimate goal. However, nothing could deter him from wanting to be with Diana.

David's obsession to be with Diana began to cause increased rifts and arguments among the three of us. Earl does not tolerate lying under any circumstances. I normally do not either. However, I was also trying to be the peacemaker. I was in the middle and it hurt. I was angry and confused. David was my son, my flesh and blood, and I wanted so much for our relationship to work. Earl felt at times that I was on David's side. My loyalties were torn. I felt frustrated. I did not like what David was doing, but I did not like how Earl was handling the situation. The tension was unbelievable. Earl was right. I just did not know how to handle the situation. I was afraid of pushing David away.

When David was away on his trips to see his friends or working, Earl and I felt relieved. We had moments of peace and temporary relaxation. I recognized that decisions would have to be made sooner rather than later. Our counselors reminded us that David was an adult. He had to make his own decisions and live with them. We did not have control over his actions – only our own.

The final straw came in December. During a break from school, David wanted to go to Florida to meet his best friend and his family who were taking a cruise. They had asked David to accompany them. That was the story. David instead spent more than two weeks with Diana and her family in Las Vegas. He said he would be back before Christmas. He returned New Year's Eve. It felt a lot like the times when Carlos showed up hours later than we agreed, called late or refused to bring the children at the last minute.

I picked David up at the airport alone. We went to La Madeleine cafe and had coffee. He talked and I listened, yet, I could tell his words were artificial. He was defensive. David really did not want to listen or understand what I was saying. He was a teenager in adult clothing. By the time we joined Earl and Monica at the special New Year's Eve dinner, David hardly spoke to me. He and Earl did not exchange one word until we left to come home. Earl did not want David to drive, and they shouted and cursed at each other. Monica now joined me in the middle. We cried.

David left after the first of the year and returned to Mexico to be with Diana. He felt that this was the only decision he could make. All plans of his becoming a commercial pilot were dropped.

He lived with her family in Cuernavaca and enrolled in college at Tec de Monterrey. Diana's mother paid for the tuition and then, through David, approved my credit card I had on file with the school to pay for his courses the first semester, without my permission. When she and I finally spoke at my insistence, she could not understand why I was upset! Unbelievable.

I was heartbroken. David had been snatched from me once again, this time by himself. I felt abandoned, helpless and even hopeless. This was not the relationship I had wanted to build.

Reflections from Earl:

David is one of those people that you love one minute and almost dislike the next. He has been lied to so much in his life that he does not understand that a lie is not going get him anyplace. I have told both Monica and David over and over that I would never lie to them. They had been lied to all their lives, but I would not lie to them. Monica got it, but not David.

David decided that he wanted to become an airline pilot and his sister, Susan and I bought into it. He did not tell any of us that he could not go back to college because of his grades.

David did most everything very well, and I was very proud of him until he got his private pilot license. Then the other David came out. It was one lie after another, two trips to Mexico behind our backs. Then came the big lie where he told us he was going to spend time with a friend in Miami, but instead he went to see his girlfriend and her family in Las Vegas.

Susan and I were so mad, hurt and every feeling that one can think of. We had had it with David and his lies. We figured that we had spent far more money on him than we ever thought (and did not have) and enough was enough.

We told him that he could no longer live with us. He could get a job, his own place to live, and still go to pilot school in Dallas or he could return to Mexico. He went back.

Over the next year and half, Monica gave him money when he did not have any and he lived with this person or another. David could not stay with anything for very long and quit jobs after just three or four months. It was rocky for a while, but things got better for him. I caught flak from friends for our tough love approach, but we felt he would never respect us or even try to stop lying to us if we didn't set a firm boundary with him.

Reflections:

- **Focus on the long-term relationship** – It may not be the ideal or desired one, the importance is that there IS a relationship that continues to build.

- **Prepare to relive important childhood stages** – I learned from therapists that I consulted that children need to relive stages of their lives that they missed with the parent left behind – no matter how old they are when found. David, for example, went through his teenage period where he had to act out and rebel against mine and Earl's parental authority.

- **Accept what is and not what could have been** – Being real and authentic underscores acceptance of the actual situation. By erasing expectations, one lives in the moment and embraces each day. Calling life the new normal puts perspective into everyday activities. As difficult as it was for all of us when David lived with us, we were finally no longer visitors with each other, being on our best behavior. Superficiality was gone, the masks taken off, exposing who we really were. This is how families are – freckles, dimples, AND warts!

- **Be patient** – Don't push for the relationship to happen. It takes time to build trust, confidence, and love. I was so anxious for Monica's time with us to work out – that she would enjoy her semester at SMU so much that she would elect to transfer and graduate here and not return to Mexico. I was looking for the perfect ending. I looked more at what I wanted rather than what Monica desired and needed. In effect, my behavior pushed her to go back to Mexico.

- **Acknowledge their culture** – Children who have been raised in a foreign culture have that as their norm now. They need time to adjust to yours. The U.S. was new to Monica and David after so much time had elapsed. They each were listening and having to speak a new language, understand new cultural mores, geography, state and federal laws, etc. In both cases, Monica and David were also studying. While I understand the Mexican culture and speak the language, I was inconsistent in helping Monica and David adjust to a new way of life.

- **Plan to be disrupted** – When a child returns after a long-term separation, there is an adjustment for the parent/family too. In my case, Earl and I had not had children living with us since we had been together. What would it be like having an adult child live with us? It is challenging even for parents whose child had not been abducted. While parenthood often seems to be a natural instinct, on the job experiences are the true learning tools. Earl and I had to adjust to being parents, he as a step-parent, a role he had never experienced. As wonderful as it was to have Monica and David living with us, Earl and I also had to plan how we would continue to live our lives. We fell into some magical thinking about how wonderful it would be without some realistic planning about how challenging it could be.

- **Treat your returning child/children normally and consistently** – Being consistent with children as they adapt to the family is vital. Monica and particularly David would try to manipulate us, thinking that we would want to do everything possible to please in order for them to like us. Establishing and maintaining consistency in our parent roles while treating both as adults contributed to earning respect. Good old fashioned boundary setting is crucial to minimize manipulation.

- **Consider therapy for the whole family** – I am a strong advocate for therapy or counseling to grow and become healthier. Therapy has helped me immensely from when Monica and David were abducted, my search for them, and since I reunited with them. Earl has reached out for support too. I always advise parents who are reuniting with their children after an abduction to seek family counseling. It is immensely valuable to the process of rebuilding a family to sit down together with a professional.

I learned this the hard way because I did not do so with Monica and David. We were not living together most of the time, which was part of the issue. The other problem was I focused on Monica and David and what I perceived as issues they had, rather than all of us as a family learning how to be a family again. I found a recommended therapist for Monica and she visited with this person a few times, but felt forced. She angrily wanted to know why she had to go. She was fine and did not need help. I learned a valuable lesson about my approach.

Other families whom I've supported have found family therapy to be a huge help. Rebuilding becomes a family project to work on together. The focus is on getting to know each other and communicate rather than talk about the abduction (unless someone wants to).

Eight

The New Normal: Monica and David

At this writing, it has been about 14 years since we found Monica and David and our lives are – happily! – very different. Last year, Monica sent a text wishing Earl and me Happy Thanksgiving. "Mom, are you spending the holiday at Mo Ranch like you do every year?" I replied, "Yes, and I wish you were here. How about catching a flight and I'll meet you in San Antonio?" My daughter answered. "Meet me at 2:00 p.m."

When I later texted her it was time to make plans for Christmas and New Year's, she said it was not important where we spent the holidays, as long as we were together! And she added a smiley face with a hug.

I am awestruck how far Monica and I have come since that tumultuous reunion in Toluca. Strangers. Acquaintances. Almost friends. Now best friends. Now mom and daughter. At what point did Monica begin to call me mom? It began with a Mother's Day greeting three years ago. The written sentiment became verbal and Monica started to say mom each time we talked and wrote. It was natural, quiet, with no fanfare. Perhaps it was her maturity and developing a sense of who she was both professionally and personally. Perhaps it was the awareness and initial understanding, and possible acceptance of what had transpired all these years. Possibly, it was my being real with her. No façade. No being on best behavior. Being truly who I am. Monica also being who she is. This year (2013) she sent me flowers for Mother's Day for the first time. I was so touched and overjoyed. For so many years, Mother's Day was a day I hid away from the world because my kids were gone, and it was a bitter day for me. Today it is sweet!

Our mother – daughter weekends acted as the catalyst for this realness. During various family trips whether to Mexico or to the U.S., Monica and I would carve time to go to a café for a cappuccino or a glass of wine. It was our moment to visit without David and Earl: Woman time together. This was the start of becoming friends and then mom and daughter. Monica would share what she was doing at work, with her friends, the books she read, and other interests on her mind at the time. I would do the same and we had wonderful conversations. During one of these visits, Monica suggested the idea of mother – daughter weekends. These would allow us to have quality time together and explore new places and surroundings. We would plan these trips – attempt at least three per year, possibly four.

How beautiful, fun, and heart-filled they have been! Monica and I have traveled to Galveston, Austin, Puerto Vallarta, and Cancun. On the planning board are Santa Fe, New Orleans, and Cabo San Lucas. Even if we do not go to these places, we will think of other locations. The most important part of these weekends is being together and sharing experiences.

During these weekends, Monica and I have discovered what it is like to confide freely and speak from the heart. We're serious at times, playful at others. We giggle, we laugh, and yes, there are tears sometimes. There is still so much I want to share that is in my heart, and I know she wants to do the same. However, we have made significant strides.

Monica currently is a brand manager for a worldwide corporation in Mexico City. She travels constantly, which she greatly enjoys. Monica is at an exciting period of her life professionally. Who knows what the future may hold.

She has a strong network of friends, and she socializes frequently. There is no significant other in her life at this time; however, she has her eye on a man she met on a business trip. Long-distance relationships are difficult, yet with matters of the heart, there are always surprises!

Monica has also considered pursuing an MBA scholarship in Spain. This is an English-speaking program, and she would specialize in international studies. One of the most attractive aspects of such an opportunity for a job transfer, I believe, would be for her to move away from family responsibilities in Mexico and live on her own.

Carlos is living with Monica and is dependent upon her for a livelihood. No longer with the state government in Toluca, he tried in vain after moving to Cuernavaca to find a similar position in the state of Morelos and in Mexico City. Carlos had hoped his brother, Ramon, would help him find a job in the government. This never transpired. His other brother, Jaime, ultimately had Carlos working with him on commission basis for sales activities in his real estate activities.

The years have been harsh on Carlos emotionally and physically. In 2007, Ramon was killed by three men in a drive-by shooting near his home. The police and newspaper reports stated that the assailants murdered Ramon to silence him regarding an arms and drug deal of which he was aware. To date, the attackers have not been found.

Since Ramon was the primary thread that held Carlos and the other immediate family members together, his death created an unraveling of the familial fabric. Carlos' strongest ally and support was gone. Although he and Jaime connected, it was not the same. Consequently, Carlos turned to Monica, in particular, for emotional support.

About a year after Ramon's death, Carlos had a stroke. Although it was mild, the stroke affected him, particularly in rapidly aging him. Since then, Carlos has had other ailments and illnesses. Through all of Carlos' calamities, Monica has been the caregiver.

Just before our mother-daughter trip to Cancun, Monica told me that something serious had happened; however, she would wait until we were together to tell me. Expecting the worst, I was extremely anxious. I learned once I met her in Cancun that Carlos had been hit by a hit-and-run driver earlier that week. Although his injuries were not life-threatening, he had fractured his arm and his body overall was badly bruised. Monica had considered not making the trip; however, she wanted to see me and reach out for support. We have truly come a long way in our relationship. Only a few years ago, Monica would have opted to stay with her father rather than make the trip to see me.

Since the abduction, Monica has been the surrogate mother and wife to her brother and father. She has been the rescuer to those nearest to her. She has not really developed a life of her own. Now that she knows I am here for her, Monica is craving the nurturing of motherly attention that she has been deprived of all these years. Monica is an adult who needs to experience the childhood stages with me she never had. I have been told by two therapists that with each visit and/or trip we do, Monica will demonstrate a different stage. While it has been difficult for me to label each stage, I do understand. Monica interacts differently with me in some ways when we are together.

Recently, Monica herself has begun to express resentment about the role she has played with her father and brother for so many years. She has expressed her need to break away and be independent. "Mom, when I am with you and Earl, I can be a daughter and not have to take care of anyone else," she cried recently when we were together. Monica acknowledged that she never really experienced being a little girl and wants so desperately to combine some of those experiences she missed with being an independent adult. How my heart ached for her! It always will.

My fervent prayers and wishes are that Monica will achieve her dreams and be happy in all areas of her life, particularly with her personal relationships. She has told me that she would like to meet someone, fall in love, get married and have children. At the same time, Monica said that if she does not meet that special person, she will be content to be who she is and achieve success in any avenues she chooses to pursue.

At 31, Monica is the same age I was when I gave birth to her. I wonder if she will have children one day. My sense is she will.

Monica has decided to buy a home in Mexico City. Part of me applauds her for taking such a big step. My other part in my heart feels sad. I so wish that she lived closer. I miss her tremendously.

Monica and I are also friends. I love when we text and talk about our crazy schedules and projects to complete. Maybe I am feeling more anxious to make up for lost time as I get older and younger simultaneously.

And maybe, just maybe, I am beginning to express my real feelings to Monica. Not being afraid to be who I am or wondering if she will love me. I know that she does. I love being her mom, and I am letting her know how much I do.

The other day I had an intuition that Monica was not doing well. Something was wrong. I texted her. She had a crisis at work that she needed to help resolve, and she had to go out of town the next day to Monterrey, where she did not want to go. Monica asked me how I knew that something was not right. I replied: Mom's intuition.

David Today:

There have been changes with David that I never would have imagined even a year and a half ago. Shortly after Christmas 2012, David told me that he had been accepted as a flight attendant for a national airline in Mexico; he had to go through a training program in Monterrey. Upon successful completion, he would be given a contract. I knew that he had gone through flight attendant training for another airline; however, he had not been accepted due to his stuttering. Earl and I were concerned that David would encounter a similar issues with this airline.

I could hear the excitement in his voice. In addition, David said that he hoped we would be proud of him. He asked if Earl was happy to hear his news and if he was proud, too. Earl sent an email where he said that he was really proud of him and wished him the best with his new job. David replied and ended his message with, "Love Son." He also called Earl "Dad." I was dumbfounded and tears rolled down my cheeks. Earl took the opportunity to reach out to David. I helped with the translations:

Hi David,

Did you ever think what the term SON means?

I have always loved you because I am in love with your mother and you are a part of her. Until now, I have loved you but I did not always like you because most everything you said or did was a lie: I have never known a man your age who had not grown up and become a man standing on his feet and being honest and understanding where other people were coming from. You have been lied to so much in your life that it became a way of life for you. Enough said, you know what I mean.

Now, I feel that you have grown into a man that I can be proud of. You have a real career. You can think and be a man of character. A man that others can look up to and say good things about.

You are starting to be the man that I was hoping that you would be. I have always wanted a son. Now, I feel that our relationship is one of a father and son.

Remember, it is so easy to fall back into old habits. I mean that it would be very easy for you to start telling lies again etc. That will get you nowhere in life because you always have to remember what you said to someone the last time. I have told you and Monica that I will never lie to you, and I never will. I don't have to worry what I have ever said before because it is always the truth. You may not like what I say, but you know it is the truth. The best way to lose a friend is to lie. I am proud to call you SON. I want to always be this proud. It is your life. Do not let yourself down and you will find me standing by you.

Love
Earl

David sent the following email:

Hi Earl

I loved your email! Really loved it! Thanks for your words! I feel too that our relationship is father and son.

Get help from Mom to read this.

(TRANSLATION FROM SPANISH)

I really like your words! Thank you very much! I also feel very proud of what we have experienced together and feel that we have all grown. For my part, believe me that I will never lie again to you both. I have matured a lot and understand what I have done; it is not like me to lie. I love you both very much, both you and my mother. Hopefully, we will see each other very soon so that we may celebrate many things. Truthfully, you have taught me a lot of things Earl, and I am able to say that I admire, respect, and love you

Love you mucho both! Special Hugs and Kisses!

With Love,
Son David

After all the heartache and stress that had happened while David was living here, and his subsequent return to Mexico where we continued having issue after issue, this was an incredible breakthrough. Earl was so touched. I had never seen him react like this; we both cried together.

David wanted to make amends for all that happened before, the lies, the heartaches. He thought that the one way to show us that he was trying to get on the right path was obtaining a job that he really wanted. Even more, David wanted Earl to be proud of him. David had never had a true male role model before he met Earl. In spite of his claims at times about his father supporting him, I just knew that David was crying for someone to want and accept him. In spite of all the harsh exchanges with Earl, at heart, Earl earned David's respect. David knows that Earl loves him unconditionally.

David knows that I do too. In some ways, David and I connect and have a bond that needs no explanation. We talk freely and effortlessly. I so wish that I would have been there for him when he was little and helped him grow. He has a sensitivity that I understand and try to nurture. I know how confused he must have been during the years that we were apart. Monica has shared that David was unlike other children, in fact, very different from others in their father's family. It was not until David grew older that she began to realize he may be more like me. Once we had reunited, Monica has said repeatedly how much David and I are alike.

I saw David during Easter weekend this year (2013) in Mexico City. This was the first time I had seen him since he had returned to Mexico after living with us. He was now working full-time. He was excited to see me and I him. I was nervous in a way, not knowing what to expect. Even though we had been communicating via text and email, we had not seen each other and really talked for a long time.

What a reunion we had! David took Monica and me out to dinner. This was a first! He planned the location and drove us. When the bill came, the look on his face when he paid was priceless! Just like the MasterCard® commercials.

Moreover, I could tell how much he enjoyed his job. David said that one day he would like to be a commercial pilot. While he had not completed his training in Dallas, he said he was determined to do so. David believes that by being a flight attendant, he will have an opportunity to achieve this. Somehow, for David, if one door did not work, another one might. This was definitely a different David from a few years ago.

Most of all, I felt a sincerity from David that I had not felt before. He truly felt sorry about the trouble he had caused us. He said that he learned some lessons, and he would never lie to us or anyone again. His focus is on his career and he is doing well to be self-sufficient. While I know he will stumble like anyone, his intentions are in the right direction and somehow or another he will achieve what he wants to do. David said that he had even learned about relationships with women. While he had friends, he was not interested in having a serious relationship at this time. One day, of course.

I also realize that David was not meant to have a college career. He is not desk nor office-oriented. He loves being free, traveling, and continually meeting new people. We may have had doubts that David really loved aviation. I really believe now that he does. To him, flying equals freedom.

I so regret David not being closer! He is a lot of fun to be with, and I enjoy being in his company. Just like with Monica, I wish he were living in the U.S. One day, though, he may have an opportunity with an airline here. Life's journeys have interesting turns and junctures.

I also ache not having more contact with him. Even though we text each other and talk occasionally, it is not the same.

David and I decided to start a tradition just like I did with Monica; a mother – son weekend. He is now based in Cancun and will be flying to Houston and San Antonio. We are scheduling a weekend. I cannot wait to have time to spend together!

I am happy to see David living away from his sister and father. He needs this independence and, I believe, has wanted to break away for a long time.

It is amazing to me to see both children creating their lives. So different yet doing so in their own ways. Monica and David are finding and experiencing the challenges of adulthood. Two very different personalities and I love watching and participating in their progress.

Monica and David's support for this book

My plans to write a book have been on the board for several years. Friends and others said before and after the kids and I reunited, "I hope you are writing down everything that has happened," and "What has happened to you would make incredible reading." Even though my thoughts and seeds to write were there, I pushed them back into my mind for a long period. It was not time. I wanted the book to be more than just a chronicle of the abduction and my locating Monica and David. There are other reunion stories out there. I wanted my story to cover what happens after the reunion and the years it takes to build a family after a long separation.

As I support other families dealing with familial abduction, I wanted to write this book for them and all the other parents/families that have experienced a long-term separation/reunification with their children for any one of various reasons, abduction, runaway, adoption, even being separated at birth. The focus would be on building the relationships and the challenges involved once the family was back together. Moreover, I wanted Monica and David along with Earl to share their perspectives. I thought their views would make the book more powerful.

When I first shared the idea with Monica. I was surprised and touched – I had so many lumps in my throat I could not talk – when she told me that she would love to write a chapter. Wow! I knew that this would be so difficult for her and doing it would take incredible courage.

When I talked with David, he agreed although at the time I do not believe he understood to what he really was agreeing. He just wanted to support me and the book project. He wanted to please me so that I would be happy. I will note here that he has been the one who is the most curious about the support I provide to families of missing children and the presentations I make on related topics.

Of the two, David has been the most idealistic about everything that has happened. A fairy tale in which everything is going to be OK and we all live happily ever. This is David's way of survival. He had been devoid of a mom and a family for so long that this is his only way to cope. Particularly with everything that we experienced together that was devastating at the moment, David does not want to lose the relationships that he has just found. He is scared to be abandoned.

Monica, being so very analytical, had a difficult time writing her chapter. When I saw her recently, we talked about the book, and I asked her questions that I thought would help her frame her thoughts. In one of the best conversations we have had, Monica expressed how angry she had been when she lived with us during her semester at SMU. She thought that we were trying to force her to stay in Dallas and not accept her for who she was. She and I both cried. We talked it through. I never understood how angry she had been during this time. I expressed how disappointed and sad I had been when she did not choose to stay in Dallas to complete her education at SMU. It was a hard conversation, so important though to say verbally all that we had been feeling. I encouraged her to include these feelings in her chapter, and I'm glad she did. Her story will help others, I just know it. She was surprised to learn that I would be OK with her expressing such feelings in the book. She is also worried that her words will be changed. I assured her that nothing will be published without her permission.

Monica is also really scared that the book will be derogatory towards her father. While I cringe when she says this, I understand. I have assured her that the focus is on building our relationships with her, David, and Earl. The book is not about her father. However, I also know that his presence is in so many of its pages. I have tried very hard to remain factual – this happened, that didn't happen – and not to make this about my anger towards him for what he did to our children and me. I know that every parent with abducted children that reads this book will know exactly how I felt during those 12 long years. What I want to show them is how to rebuild afterwards: how to be realistic and patient when reuniting with your child.

I am in awe that both Monica and David's viewpoints will be in my book! It is incredible….I cannot put into words how I feel about them agreeing to be included. My heart bursts when I think about how far we have all come. I am brimming with feelings, thoughts….what a dream. And to think not very long ago, the three of us never thought we would be friends, let alone mother, daughter, son.

Reflections on how to keep building:

- **Stay real –** To accept a relationship for what it is without unrealistic expectations is even more important now than in the early years after reuniting. As the relationship builds and expands, you might feel comfortable, so it is easy to fall back and think there will never be any more challenges/disappointment. Celebrate the successes and know that there will be ebbs and flows.

- **Go with the flow –** It is important to continually nurture the relationship and go with the flow while life's events occur. Both Monica and David are adults now and need to live their own lives. I do not possess them, I just want to participate and be a mother/friend in their lives.

- **Communicate** – One of the wonderful aspects of technology is that Monica, David, and I are able to text frequently. We connect. Even though we express that we love each other, send hugs and kisses, it is the thought behind the text that truly matters. We are thinking about each other when we communicate this way. Except for when we see each other in person and are able to truly converse, this communication reflects so often real feelings about what is happening in our lives. Even phone calls, while wonderful to hear each other's voices, are sometimes difficult. We seem hesitant to really talk. I don't know really why, yet I think I understand. Monica, I know, will call or I will call when she is at home. Since her father is living with her, I am never sure even at this point in her life how comfortable she is in talking about certain subjects. When we are together, she truly confides. David is more open. It does not bother him that someone is around although I can tell when he has a serious topic to discuss, he is not comfortable at times talking. I know then that someone is around he does not want to hear what he is saying.

- **Let go –** There will always be painful barriers in the relationship. I wasn't there when my children needed me, and they're angry about it. I took too long to find them. I died and then came back. I abandoned them (according to their father). The children have a lot of confusing and irrational feelings that must be addressed in a kind and loving way. It is not fair, but I had to drop my need to be right or to explain or to justify my actions in order to build a relationship with David and Monica. The shadow of Carlos lingers. He is Monica and David's father. His influence on them is still there and always will be. The key is to let go and accept what is. I love my children. Our relationship ultimately is what counts in my life.

- **Laugh –** A sense of humor will help you get through a lot of rough spots in the process. Laughing and having fun together helps with bonding. It also helps get through mistakes and awkward moments lightly. It is easy for things to become heavy pretty fast since there are a lot of big emotions at play. Joking and trying not to take things too seriously can help.

Nine

Monica's Story

M*onica's perspective on where we are today as a family:*

If you met me today, you might think I am a very lucky person. A 31-year-old marketing executive, working for one of the most important companies worldwide with my own apartment and traveling internationally several times a year sounds cool. You would see immediately that even though I am not a very extroverted person, I love to smile and really enjoy a good joke. If we spent a little bit more time together, you would know how much I love coffee, how much I enjoy reading good books, how deeply I respect and admire scientific matters, how much I like sports, and how much I am secretly in love with Roger Federer.

After some time together, you would know about my amazing and fun friends who make me laugh every day with their jokes through our chat on Whatsapp, our fun travels to cities in Mexico, our funniest videogame afternoons, and how we try to fix the world so easily every week with a good bottle of wine or exotic drinks. Certainly, after all of that, you will say I am pretty lucky person.

After even more time you may become my friend, and then you would get to know my admirable and lovely mother, my amazing and caring father and my exceptional and good-hearted brother. Only then you would understand how deeply I love them, how much I enjoy spending time with them and how grateful I am to have them in my life. Only then you would understand that all the things that I have achieved and made me the person who I am today are a result of their love.

Our journey together hasn't been easy at all, and it took years to have the relationships we have today. Everything we passed through, though, has been worth it.

Why didn't the relationship between my parents work? I certainly don't know. Would it have been better for the four of us if they had chosen to stay together? I don't know either. Probably not. I had a wonderful childhood and I am so grateful for that. I remember how my dad got up every day at 5:00 a.m. to make us breakfast, to get our clothes washed and to get my brother and me ready to leave. After taking us to school, he drove to his job, worked all morning, and picked us up for lunch while he asked how our day was. He tried to teach us new things in that short time. He'd leave us home safely and run again to get to his job, probably making up some story about how he went to see a client to avoid getting fired.

At night, he tried to get home very early to give us dinner, play and talk with us. On weekends, he was always taking us to places we wanted: the park, the movies, to practice some sport (I think because of that, I am a very athletic person). He did this every week for years. Once a friend asked him: "Are you insane? You can't do this alone. Being a single mother is difficult, but being a single father is twice as hard. You really need a partner and to do things with adult people. Why don't you get a girlfriend or something?" I still admire his response: "I don't want to give somebody else the time I want to give to my children. I really enjoy spending time with them. They need me as much as I need them."

I was always kind of shy but had good friends in elementary school and high school. I started my passion for reading when I was 12 years old with the Swedish novel *The Wonderful Travel of Nils Holgerson*, and since then, I haven't stopped reading every night. I was always good with sports, so I practiced a lot of them all my childhood and youth.

As the older sister, I was always responsible for my brother. I taught him a lot of things and took care of him. That built a close, strong and deep relationship between us. Now I can happily say that I contributed to the person he has become today: an intelligent and excellent human being.

When I was 17, I remember one day a lady asking for me while I was in class. She said my mom wanted to see my brother and me. After the shock, I decided to see her. This lady arranged the meeting in a hotel. I don't think my brother remembered her, but I did when I saw her after all of those years. It was very impactful. What can you say to someone you haven't seen since you were 5 years old? I don't remember having at that moment any strong feelings for her, no hate, love, guilt or regret. I was only curious and trying to be nice. We saw her several times after that day. Everything was nice and kind. She was a very lovely and cheerful lady. One day, she introduced us to her husband, a fun and tall guy, with a deep voice. Even when he didn't speak a lot, I remember I liked him.

Some years passed that way: they used to come to Mexico once or twice a year for a few days. We went to cool places, first only with her, then with both of them. We had fun, we talked about easy things and enjoyed the time together. After several years, I really liked her and her husband, and I started to think I could trust them like very good friends.

My college allowed some students to study in other countries in order to have international experience. Even when my dad couldn't afford the tuition, he enrolled me there because he wanted me to have an excellent education. I got good grades to be a scholarship candidate, which helped my dad with the bills. After some semesters, my mom agreed to help with my tuition. I will always be grateful to her for that. One way to express my gratitude was to maintain high grades. Those good grades and the fact that I became President of the Marketing Students Association made me eligible to study in the U.S. or Europe. Fortunately, one of the colleges within this agreement was Southern Methodist University in Dallas, Texas. That was the perfect opportunity to have my international experience, to enrich my resume, but most importantly, to really get to know my mom.

Living in a different country with a different culture, behaviors and language is difficult. Getting to know your mom and parts of your life you hardly remember made it a completely unknown experience. I really didn't know what to expect. The only thing I knew at that time was that it would be something very exciting, fun and enriching in every single way. I was going to live with my mom and Earl, which made me happy. I would get to know both of them better, how they lived, and learn how to strengthen our relationship which I thought was very good. I went to Dallas with a lot of hope. Big mistake. It wasn't perfect and happy at all and certainly we didn't become better friends.

At the beginning, everything was very wonderful: new country, new home, new family and new school. I remember how nicely my mom and Earl received me. A beautiful room, flowers, two lovely cats. I felt so touched. Earl made wonderful dinners with long and nice talks each evening. They took me on a lot of incredible trips to have fun together. They were always thinking of how to make me happy. Also, I was studying in one of the most important universities in Texas, a place where a lot of people really want to go, with excellent teachers and great activities for international students. What went wrong then?

Simple: neither of us knew at that time how to build a parent-daughter relationship within our past. Both sides had a past that we didn't share together at all and a past that didn't know anything about the other side. We just assumed that the correct way of living was ours and our own past was the right thing, and the other person was wrong. We tried so hard to convince the other side that we were right and the only way to be happy was making the other accept and embrace that reality. We just forgot, or wanted to forget that the other side had a past, links, and previous experiences without the other person. Not living them together was neither wrong nor right. It was just the way it was.

It was really painful for me to hear how they referred to my dad so severely, without knowing that he is such a wonderful father and one-in-a-million. At the same time, I can imagine now how painful it was dealing with such an immature and close-minded person, only thinking about herself and trying to make things just the way she wanted, without putting herself in the other side's shoes. After some months, it was very hard to speak with them without fighting so I decided to stay longer at school studying. But when you feel so lonely, when you can't speak the language fluently, and when you don't have really good friends there, you start to fail in your grades. I hardly finished that semester and only because I wanted to get back with my dad, my brother, my friends and the school I enjoyed so much. So I left immediately after I finished, thinking that I was never to speak with them again.

The time back in Mexico helped me a lot to put things in perspective. After some time, I decided to start again. This time without judging, forcing, and trying to keep an open mind. But most importantly, trying to be empathetic and respectful to them, and understanding that even when we didn't share part of our lives together, we can surely share the rest of it. I realized that after all we had been through, the most important thing was: we are family. No matter all the problems, we will be always there for each other. I think my mom realized that too at the same time because suddenly everything just got better very easily. After that, I could do something I never did before: I called her "mom."

My relationship with Earl changed too. After being just my mom's husband, now he is my spiritual guide. I can't see him as a parent, but as the best guide someone can have. I respect him so deeply that I always ask him when I want to talk with someone wise and smart. I appreciate his lovely and wise advice and understand why my mom chose him to share her life. We share so much in common (like the fact we prefer reading a good book with a glass of wine rather than going to a party or speaking on the phone like my mom and brother), and we have a strong bond together.

Ten years have passed since then and now I can surely tell you that I have the perfect family. My relationship now with my mom is so healthy, full and significant that I enjoy all the time we spend together. Our mom & daughter weekends mean a lot to me because it helps us to share special moments and thoughts together, allowing me to know her better and respect her more each day for what she is and what she has accomplished in her life.

I am totally happy with my relationship with my two parents, each of them with their own personality, culture and even sense of humor. Each of them has taught me many important invaluable lessons, and I am so thankful for that.

After meeting me this way, as I said before, you might think I am a very lucky person, but I am not lucky. I am blessed.

Reflections on Monica's Story

The moment I received Monica's email with her story, I started trembling. Each time I read it, I cried. I probably cried more than over any part of the chapters I have written. My heart was aching and vibrating for her, for David, for me, and for Earl.

I knew that Monica would write her perspective this way. She has been so afraid that my book would portray her father as an evil man, and she does not want any words said that would even hint at this. She loves him, and she is stuck in the middle.

I am also feeling sick. When Monica mentions that she loves her father's response about "the children need him as much as he needs them," and not needing anyone else to divert his attention, I am repulsed. How sick! So unhealthy…it goes above and beyond unhealthy.

The image of him as a struggling single dad is astonishing to me, too. He wouldn't have been a single dad if he hadn't left me and stolen the kids. It defies belief.

There is a part of me that so badly wants my children to understand. It is hard to accept that it may never happen and to let go of this desire. This is some of the tough news I have for parents who are reuniting with their children after a long separation – your child may never understand what you went through and how hard you worked to get them back. Your child will probably continue to love the other parent…and it's not their fault.

So many feelings, and I know I am playing head vs. heart games. Intellectually, I get what Monica and David are going through. I have supported enough families who have experienced family abductions that I understand why abducted children act like they do. If they admit to being abducted and acknowledge lies the abducting parent told them, they have to admit that much of their lives have been lies. That's the head of reason talking. It is not the same with my heart.

Monica's letter gives insight into her life without a mom, taking care of her brother. I found it interesting that she talked so casually about her father telling stories to the workplace about being with a client when he was having lunch with them. He made lying seem heroic. I imagine they saw their dad tell lots of stories which is perhaps why honesty is such a tough issue with David.

She really nailed it on the head when she talked about how, "We just assumed that the correct way of living was ours and our own past was the right thing, and the other person was wrong." I wanted my children to see things my way. They wanted me to accept that their father was a good guy who took care of them. We may never agree about Carlos, but our relationship together is more important than that and is growing despite that fact.

The reasons we were able to start again after Monica left was because 1) she wanted to and 2) Earl and I backed off from talking about the abduction. I sincerely hope that Monica talks with a professional one day about her childhood, but I recognize that it can't be me. I'm her mom, not her analyst. I'm here to be with her and share her life, not pick it apart.

Today, Monica loves me and that is overwhelmingly precious to me. I know it was painful for her to write her perspective and I'm grateful. I think her words will help other families.

Since I received her chapter, I have told her how much I love her and value her thoughts. It is time for a mother-daughter weekend. I want to give her multiple hugs and really talk. I want to break down more barriers.

Ten

David's Story

David's perspective on where we are today as a family, translated from Spanish:

I wanted to see my mom again. I was a baby the last time I saw her. My hope when I saw her again was to get to really know her, to have a mother-son relationship and to be able to be a family. My second hope was that she would accept me, love and acknowledge me as her son because we had not had contact with her in such a long time.

The first time I saw her, I was nervous. I did not know if she really loved me, wanted to hug me, or wanted me. I did not know what she thought about me. I wanted to hug her and start our new relationship.

When we had dinner together that first time I was happy because I realized that she loved me, wanted me and would always be by my side going forward.

Fortunately, my biological father always said very good things about my mom so I always had a positive impression about her. I was so surprised, though, when my mom told me why she was unable to see us for such a long time. I suspected; however, I wanted to hear directly from her. The other surprise was how my mom had changed physically from the old photos I had seen. She is still beautiful.

To me, it is very important to have a family. It is the basis of being human. The family represents the only pure love and affection in your life. Your family helps you grow and always gives you support.

Through the love and support of my family, I am able to grow and be motivated to be a better person each day.

For me, my family is my mother, sister, Dad Earl, and my father. We have grown together and learned from one another. Even though there were obstacles and rocks in the road, the most important thing is that we confronted and resolved these problems together.

Overall, I feel really good about my parents. I love my mom and father a lot. The problems they had are separate from my relationship with each one. Obviously, I would have liked that they could have stayed together; however, I have been able to separate those problems from our relationship. I know they will always love and support me.

I feel good about my relationship with Earl. When I first met him, I was scared. Would he accept me and did he love my mom? After time passed, I realized I liked him and knew that he loved my mom. They are happy, which makes me happy. Earl is a great person. I have learned so much from him. We have a father-son relationship. He knows how much I love and respect him, and I know he loves me. We will always be there for each other.

I hope that mom, Dad Earl, and I will always be a family filled with love and support. A few years ago I lied to my mom and Earl. My behavior was immature and I was thinking only about what I wanted, not what others felt. I apologized to mom and Earl and asked them for forgiveness. I regret the mistakes I made in the past. Today I look at things differently. Together with my family, we grow and learn from each other. As my mom once said, through problems we grow closer and become united as a family. I love Mom and Earl Dad so very much!

At this moment, my focus is to develop myself professionally and personally. One day, I would like to get married and have children. Because I feel so strongly about the importance of a family, I want to give whomever I marry and my children the benefits and experiences that I have had with my own family.

Reflections on David's Story

In a curious way, David's perspective did not surprise me. He has an idealistic view of family and views relationships simplistically and superficially.. David's personality as I have come to know him, is to please everyone. As he and I did not have an established bond prior to the abduction and were truly starting from scratch when we reunited, David does not have history or prior perceptions.

Within his story, I feel though, his sadness and insecurity. And his sensitivity. All he wants is to be loved. It hurts me to the core as I read his thoughts the emptiness and loneliness he felt all the years we were not together. David was blessed having Monica there to help him grow and learn. Yet, my absence affected him in ways that he nor I may ever understand. His words somehow reveal a deeper issue that I cannot identify. Intuition tells me there is something behind or underneath what he is saying. I am disturbed and very concerned.

What heartens me is his growing love and acceptance towards Earl. In turn, David feels accepted and loved by him. It has been extremely important for David to gain Earl's trust and love. This has been his goal and he is succeeding. David has needed a dad in his life who accepts him the way he is and he is achieving this goal.

David and I are very much alike. Abandonment is a huge issue for both of us. He is afraid of losing the family he has now gained and in many ways, so am I. I feel that because of our personality similarities, we will continue to grow and foster our relationship to establish an unbreakable bond.

Reflections from a Stepparent

Earl shares the lessons he's learned as a Stepparent:

Monica has come a long way and has much to be proud about. Her education, her work accomplishments, her friends and her relationships with Susan and me are a testament to her warm heart, brains and strong work ethic.

It is hard for me that she won't admit that her father kidnapped her and lied to her about Susan being dead. I feel protective of Susan and want to pick apart things that aren't true in Monica's chapter. I also feel protective of Monica and wish I could help her step away from her father and be her own person. Monica is the kind of woman that feels that she can take care of the world and everything will be OK. Monica lets her father live with her and she pays for most of everything. She does not realize that even though she is in her 30's, he is still running her life in so many ways.

David still prefers to see the abduction like a messy divorce. He learned to lie from his father and didn't understand why it is wrong. For a long time, he got himself into trouble and expected others to bail him out like all those text messages he kept sending asking for money. Like his father, he relied on Monica for support when he was strapped for money. He had trouble staying with anything for very long. In these ways he reflected his father's bad habits and bad behaviors.

And yet David can be very warm and charming. He is sincere about wanting to be a family. He is growing up. He now has a real career as a flight attendant for a Mexican airline and seems to really enjoy it. We talk about honesty and he is working to break old habits. In this he is very different from his father. While I question the statement that Carlos has always said good things about Susan, I recognize that David, like Monica, is not ready to look at the lies his father told him yet.

What I'm learning is that it may always be this way. Both children have had the opportunity to learn about what happened to their mother and them for 12 years of their lives. When they are ready to talk about it, we'll be here. In the meantime we build the best relationship that we can on new experiences, the new normal of our family.

Being a stepparent is one hell of a job. You try to do what any parent would do, but you always have to remember that you are not the father. I wish that we had found Monica and David at least ten years earlier. I could have been a positive male role model for David.

Today I feel that both of them love me and that I am a part of their lives. Being a stepparent, I am the only one that can walk away and go on with my life. However, they are (in my mind) my children, and I want the best for them. I want us to be a real family.

To anyone who is a stepparent, here's what I've learned about being a stepparent over the past 14 years:

- Let your partner, the parent, do most of the talking. You are in a support role.

- Keep your mouth shut, listen and watch body language.

- Be a friend and just a friend.

- After you are a friend, you can start acting like a parent without being perceived to be an outsider.

- Use tough love if you have to, but remember you are the stepparent.

Eleven

The New Normal: Susan and Earl

November 2, 1987 was so long ago, yet I have moments when it is like yesterday. The feelings, oh those feelings of disbelief, heartache, pain, betrayal, abandonment. I still see myself screaming in that hotel crying for my children. I still see Monica and David as they were before the abduction. What would their lives have been like if the children had not been abducted? My life? Of course, I will never know.

What I do know is that my love for both has and never will waver. In fact, it is deeper and more profound today than it ever has been. Of course, people would say that after going through the years of searching and finally finding Monica and David, my love for them has truly been tested and affirmed. "You never know what you have until it is gone," is the adage. This is true; however, I believe a mother knows what she has the moment her child is born. There is no love that is stronger or deeper. The bond is forever. Monica and David are part of me and always will be. Being snatched away should never have happened. There is no justification. The impact on their lives, my life, Earl's, family and friends is too great.

I believe that my relationship with Monica and David is stronger than many parents have with their adult children. We've had to work so hard at it. Nothing is taken for granted.

Today, Monica, David, Earl, and I have our story. We have the new normal relationship. Both Monica and David are in Mexico. They are working, have their friends and activities. We keep in touch via text, calls, emails and plan trips to get together. Do Earl and I wish they lived close by? Of course. That is the not the way it is though. In a strange and beautiful way, I feel more connected to Monica and David than if they lived around the corner and if I saw them more frequently. There is not a day that goes by that I do not think about them, and I believe they do the same. Our hearts are together. Sometimes I will wonder what Monica or David is doing at the moment and a text will arrive. It has been fun sharing activities that we all are doing. Simple things, not spectacular, but reinforcing our bond. It is also fun. I have noticed just recently, that Monica and I will share some things together that David and I would not and vice versa. We exchange photos. We laugh through our texts and emails.

I wish my parents were still alive to be part of the relationship Earl and I now have with Monica and David. This book has been hard to write partly because mom and daddy are no longer here. I still want so much to show both of them that I did it. I hope they would be proud of me and their beautiful grandkids.

Daddy passed away in November, 1990. We were in the midst of searching for Monica and David. Daddy never even met Earl. He knew about him, that was all. The irony of it will always be with me. November 2 was Daddy's birthday. I am sure Daddy thought about that when Monica and David were abducted. Daddy had his own demons and struggles that he never resolved. He had been abandoned by his mother when he was four years old. His father had died when he was a baby. His mother returned to his life when he was 14. He lived with his grandparents and grew up believing them to be his true parents. I can only imagine how he felt when Monica and David were abducted. I ache so much wishing that he and I had been able to talk about everything and truly connect. So, so sad.

In January 2006, mom passed away. She was in Hendersonville, North Carolina, living in the same house she and Daddy had retired to in the late 1970's. I was there when she died. Earl and Cheryl's family were all there. Mom was 89, almost 90. She had had good health for the most part until six months before her death. The last time Earl and I saw and visited with her was Christmas 2005. We had a good visit. However, Mom's focus was on herself and not what we were doing. She asked few questions about Monica and David and never said she would like to see them. The door was shut on any emotions about her grandchildren and had not really changed since Monica and I saw her three years before. I felt sad and wanted to cry; however, I could not. Where were the words and feelings when I wanted them? Where Mom seemed to connect with me was my relationship with Earl. When we said goodbye at the end of our visit, mom told Earl and me to take good care of each other.

I miss dearly two very close friends, Carolyn and Liz, who are no longer here. They are irreplaceable. They both were so supportive of me and were always there. Moreover, they were advocates for missing children and efforts to bring them home. Carolyn and Liz both met Monica while she was studying at SMU. They loved her. Their lives ended way too soon.

Friendships old and new continue to be very important in my new normal life. The connections between friends and the rebuilding of my relationships with Monica and David have become stronger. I have been reminded repeatedly how necessary it is to nurture these friendships and not to forget who the true friends are. When I attended my 45th high school reunion this year, I reunited with old friends and created a connection with those I barely knew in high school.

Self-care, physical and emotional, is a huge priority. I am busier with work and activities than I ever was and am really enjoying life in this regard. I work out faithfully with a personal trainer every week. Dirk is a special person and a good trainer. We have become friends, and I so appreciate his guidance and friendship. Both Monica and David know and like him. David keeps track of my workouts; he wants to be sure that I do not give up. It is too important for my health. Both kids love and admire my energy. They also talk about their friends' parents and how different they are, how aged they have become. I tell Monica and David I am not a "sit in a rocking chair" mama nor will I ever be the grandma knitting booties for her grandchildren one day! They roll their eyes yet say they want to introduce me to their friends.

I am growing in ways that I do not realize, becoming stronger, and I like what I am feeling and seeing. Perhaps it is the writing of this book. This has been a dream of mine to do and is now a passion to complete. It is becoming real. What lies ahead is both exciting and scary. I am ready.

Earl and I have settled into a busy and active lifestyle. With his antique business, we have opportunities to travel and participate in shows. We still like to explore new places. We continue our travel traditions of attending music festivals and our Thanksgiving celebration at Mo Ranch in Hunt, Texas. New towns and locations keep beckoning, and we escape when we can create those get-away times. Earl does not believe in retirement and neither do I. There is still too much to see and do. Besides, as Earl is quick to point out, the journey with Monica and David always has a new chapter and always will. Who would want to miss any moment?!

Our advocacy and support activities for missing children have intensified during the last ten years. This is a spiritual mission for both Earl and me. We believe fervently in reaching out to support other parents and families, particularly those who have experienced abductions by family members. We are actively involved with a national telephone support group which is part of a large national organization that focuses on missing children.

When I first started searching for Monica and David, I tried to locate a support group for families affected by family or similar abductions. No luck at all. There were support groups for grief recovery and divorce; however, members did not understand what I was going through. They had not walked in my steps.

Many parents live with guilt and denial after their children are abducted. Others are afraid to talk publicly about the abduction. Even when parents are reunited with their children, they face challenges they had not expected. A support group that focuses on understanding and being there for these parents is vital. Not only do they find comfort with those who get it, they are able to validate their feelings.

Earl and I started a support group in 1993 in Richardson, Texas. We met every Saturday morning at a church. To promote awareness, we posted an announcement in local papers, including the *Dallas Morning News,* and spread the word through church members, friends, and business colleagues. As the Internet was in its infancy, of course, we did not have the social media opportunities we have today.

Our group lasted about a year. At any given time, we had 12-15 members. While the group was small, it was loyal and the members seemed to derive value from the weekly discussions. We even had media coverage about our group. A reporter with the *Dallas Morning News* wrote a story; I was interviewed by a reporter from a Dallas TV station.

The group would have continued to meet and we would have formalized to non-profit status except for a tragedy that befell one of our members. One mother located and was reunited with her two children in North Carolina. The abducting father was arrested and extradited back to Dallas. He was remanded to jail until a court hearing. The judge for unknown reasons released him. The abductor then unsuccessfully attempted to find the mother and the children.

When he failed, he decided to go after the mother's parents instead and went to their lake house where he waited in the nearby woods. When the mother's father appeared, the abductor shot and killed him.

The mother, her children, and other family members went into hiding and left the Dallas-Fort Worth area. We never received further word from them. It was a sobering reminder of what's at stake and exactly the kind of person a child abductor can be. Earl and I met with the other members of the support group and, collectively, decided that it was in the best safety interest and well-being of everyone if we disbanded the meetings. We all felt the loss tremendously.

I became aware of the support group in which Earl and I currently participate shortly after reuniting with Monica and David. This group was a lifesaver to me. After such a long separation, I needed understanding support and guidance. A few years later, the director asked me if I would like to become a volunteer with the group. I went through training, became a volunteer, and two years later agreed to be coordinator/now consultant overseeing the family abduction team (domestic and international). I will never forget the first evening of my training when the volunteers in training were asked to tell their stories. Even though I had found Monica and David and was in the process of building a relationship, I felt immediately at home. It was the first time I truly felt free to tell my story. I knew that everyone there would understand. It was incredibly liberating. I had found a family who cared, accepted me, and would always be there. They got it.

Earl joined the support group a year after I went through training and decided to become a volunteer too. As a stepparent, Earl feels he provides strong insight and support, particularly for those who are significant others to parents whose children have been abducted.

David, Susan and Monica – reunited at last!

David and Monica Today

David and Susan

(from left to right): Monica, Susan, Earl and David

Monica and Susan's "Mother-Daughter" Weekend

Epilogue:

The journey of the heart has no ending. There is no bow that we tie and close a box and say "the trip is over." Whether the journey is going well or experiencing bumps, it keeps going. The high moments, the hiccup moments. There is always a new chapter, a new moment about to unfold. There will always be new moments with Monica and David. And I know that some of these will be difficult and challenging. Yet, there will be others that will open opportunities to become closer with each other. Even more trusting and loving. These positive moments will supersede the negative times.

The abduction changed my life forever. It changed Monica and David's too. Earl's as well. It will always be with us and has become part of the fabric of who we are as individuals and as a family.

Yet, during the last year, there has emerged a naturalness in the way all of us now interact as a family, particularly in the way Monica, David, and I communicate with each other. Even when doing something as simple as a text, I feel the spontaneity. David will check in and ask how a work project is going or send me a photo of a new restaurant that he and his girlfriend like. I do the same with him. Monica sends me a text with a "Hi FM (Favorite Mom)! How is your day going?" or I will send her one saying, "Happy Friday, FD (Favorite Daughter)! Have a beautiful day!" There is no hesitancy as to what to say with any of the three of us.

Monica visited us recently and we had the mother-daughter moments that I will always cherish. Each morning we had a chat before breakfast in my home office. Monica came in sleepy-eyed, we grabbed some coffee and she curled up on the comfy red couch. I put my feet up on the couch and we talked about anything that came to mind. Spontaneous topics. One morning Monica asked me what I was thinking and I looked at her and said, "I am so happy you're here." She looked back directly at me and answered, "So am I, Mom."

Twelve

Stories from the Kidnapped Files

Awareness about parent and related abductions is limited. Even though the public hears stories about some abductions like the father who struggled for a long time to recover his son from Brazil, most people are unaware of the impact these abductions have and the challenges that follow once families are reunited.

While it is virtually impossible to tell who will become a child abductor (unless they've done it before, of course), there are some things that families can do to make it harder for the abductor:

1) Fingerprint your kids and keep the prints in a safe place

2) Obtain certified birth certificates and keep them in a safe place where your spouse can't get them.

3) Let schools know who can remove your kids and what to do if they are removed unexpectedly.

4) Note and photograph all birthmarks.

5) If old enough, have the child(ren) memorize all your contact information.

6) Tell your family and friends not to let your children leave their care without calling you if they are watching them.

7) Make sure you have certified copies of your children's passports. If abducted, you can have your children's passports flagged.

Often I am brought in to consult with families regarding reunification issues. Parents are upset because their child doesn't call them "Mom" or "Dad" any more. They don't know how to act with their children, their kids have changed a lot and/or they are being cold and indifferent. Their children are angry, sad and afraid. Their children are strangers. My job is to help parents understand how normal all this is and how to help their kids adjust.

I offer guidance on how to open communications and safe early topics like hobbies, interests, friends and school. I suggest ways that parents can have fun with their kids with no expectations. We talk about commonalities that parents can point to between the children and themselves like their looks, smiles, gestures and more.

For the older children there are a lot of ways they may be affected. Some have trouble forming relationships. Many feel isolated from their peers because they are different. They might feel abandoned or unaccepted. Many express like Monica that they never really had a childhood. Many feel neglected and unlovable. These kids are survivors but they've been alone for too long. They need their families to help them come in from the cold.

The following stories represent some of the families with whom I support and the types of issues faced by parents left behind and their children.

Take My Kids...Please

Given how hard and long I waited to find Monica and David, I can appreciate parents who feel despair or that maybe they should give up. It astonished me, then, when I met a parent who was ambivalent about getting his children back. The wealthy mother had taken them to Mexico and he didn't want to make waves to find them. In fact, his driving force in pursuing them at all seemed to be that he wanted his kids back so they could play with his new girlfriend's kids. This was one dysfunctional family, but I felt sorriest for the children.

"Friend Me"

One parent knew where his daughter was but the mother blocked all communications. He never gave up. He ended up finding her on Facebook one day and made a friend request. Their relationship proceeded only on Facebook for a long time. She confided in him about issues with her mother during the rebellious teenage years, and he became a true friend to her. Now she is finally coming for a visit and is going to stay with him. She's 18, and it has been 16 years since she's seen her dad in person.

You're Not My Mom!

This is always so hard for freshly reunited parents to hear from their children! One mom has this in spades. Her daughter won't hug her or call her Mom, which is hard, and refuses to acknowledge her parental authority. The daughter is angry that her mom was away for so long and even angrier to find out that she has a new half-sister to boot. Mom got remarried in the waiting years and had another daughter which is infuriating to the daughter who feels replaced and unwanted (despite all facts to the contrary). While she is wanted, she is also undeniably a distraction to a family that had its routines and now suddenly has an angry teenager in the house.

This family also has large cultural issues since the daughter was abducted to Iran when she was 10 and now she is 19. Her mom is a successful doctor in America which is not a traditional job for Iranian women. In short, it's messy. Rebuilding is going to take a lot of work, time and patience.

Tapped Out

Another issue not talked about enough is how much it can cost to get your kids back. Even if you avoid the shady guys who want $200,000, you are still going to spend a lot on lawyers, private investigators, travel and other expenses – tens of thousands to hundreds of thousands of dollars sometimes. One dad I'm currently supporting is frustrated because he is tapped out. He's tried everything he can. He's spent all he can. He feels angry, depressed and full of despair. Time is ticking by, and he is impotent to do anything.

At times like this – of which I had my share – faith is the only thing you have to keep you going. My work with him is about keeping the faith. I help him see the things that are going right in his life that he can appreciate until something happens. He has a job he likes, and he has family support, including two older children. When he loses faith, I try to help him find it again. In a case like this, my 12-year+ search encourages someone else. When I tell him it can still happen he knows it is true because it happened to me.

I share these examples from real families not only to shed light on an important issue concerning our children and families, but also to provide hope. Most of the families I support have recovered or do recover their children during our time together. For all the challenges of rebuilding trust, friendships and relationships, it is worth it. Our kids are back and there's nothing more important than that.

There are many more international laws, resources, tools and support available than when my children were taken. In the appendices I've listed some of these resources to help parents and family members who have been left behind and/or have reunited with their children. In addition, I've also listed volunteer opportunities for those who, like me, feel passionately about familial abductions – both stopping them and helping families recover from them.

Appendix A: Cultural Differences Between Mexico and The United States

I made the mistake early on of minimizing or discounting the cultural differences between the U.S. and Mexico. The children were affected in many ways that would have made more sense to me at the time if I had been attuned to the differences. The list below is what I learned about my children's culture over time. If your children were taken to other countries, read through this list and think about how it might apply to your situation. Cultural experiences and understandings are largely unconscious. Your children will express them without necessarily knowing why. It is just the way things are for them. It can cause significant conflict and misunderstandings when they come home.

- Families are traditionally very close and insular in Mexico. They stick together no matter the circumstances. When Monica was here for the semester at SMU, she considered that her real family was her father, brother, and father's family. Earl and I were not family to her, particularly Earl, as he was not blood related. She felt he had no right to talk about her father or any family member. As Monica was not yet ready to verbally call me mom, I was a marginal family member. After many years, this has changed. Today, both Monica and David consider Earl and me as family.

- Monica and David are both accustomed to the class system in Mexico and each had challenges in accepting the differences in the U.S. For example, Monica did not like associating with many Mexicans in the U.S. even though she speaks Spanish.

- Although there is a growing middle class in Mexico, it is not nearly the size it is in the U.S. Historically, professional and upper class/wealthy solely connected with each other and did not step down in class. Although Monica's father and family are not wealthy, she is a professional, which distinguishes her from the working class. That being said, the culture in Mexico is transforming, according to authors, such as Luis de la Calle and Luis Rubio, in their book, "Mexico: A Middle Class Society" *Poor No More, Developed Not Yet.* There are numerous writings today about such a transformation.

- During the time David lived with us, he was not comfortable dating women who were servers in restaurants or similar occupations. As a result, even if a woman was nice to him or he thought she was cute, he would avoid further interaction. Moreover, David did not understand the concept of working in college as this is not common in Mexico for university students to do.

- Monica believes in women's rights particularly in business; however, she lacks the independent spirit prevalent with women in the U.S. She has been struggling with this cultural difference – part of her wants to be independent; the other part is a magnet connected to Mexico. She recognizes that women in the U.S. enjoy more opportunities and think more on their own. As Monica has matured professionally and personally, she is exploring opportunities for an independent work and life style.

- It was typically customary in Mexico that few individuals and families sought counseling/therapy when undergoing emotional issues. Today, that practice is changing and counseling is becoming more accepted. There were and still exist several reasons for the unwillingness to seek therapy: 1) people feel their family members can help them with problems; 2) people do not like to share their problems with strangers even those they are paying for services – it is a matter of personal pride; and 3) Cost – counseling services are expensive and deemed a frivolous expense. For both Monica and David, it is a difficult concept to understand that in the U.S., we seek counseling to resolve issues that will help us grow and become healthy.

- Monica and David both have learned the importance of serving in the community and helping others in the U.S. although this custom is not common in Mexico. That being said, they are seeing some similar movement in Mexico, particularly with health-related issues. It took time for them to understand the different causes and organizations in the U.S. and they seem to embrace the custom even if not totally understanding the energy people here exert to serve in their communities.

Appendix B: Challenges Getting Passports For The Children

My children were technically dual-citizens which actually made getting passports for them harder, not easier. Each country is different, of course, but be aware that the process may take longer than you think.

Monica

As Monica was born in Mexico City, she was Mexican by birth although she had two nationalities because of me. Prior to her coming to the U.S. to attend the semester at SMU, we wanted to obtain a U.S. passport.

We went to the U.S. Embassy in Mexico City to obtain Monica's passport. Upon arriving, we were asked numerous questions. I had to prove I was her mother with my birth certificate, tax statements, utility bills (to demonstrate I was a resident and actually living in the U.S.) and two letters from a professional colleague and personal friend. It required two trips to the Embassy, including my having to return to the U.S., obtain documents, and make another trip back to Mexico City and the Embassy in order to present the required documentation in person. We ultimately obtained Monica's passport and I thought that she would be the most difficult of both children in terms of the passports since she was not born in the U.S. I was wrong.

David

Prior to David initiating aviation school, we went again to the U.S. Embassy in Mexico City to obtain his U.S. passport. We thought that it would be easier to obtain than Mexican documents since David was born in Dallas.

When we arrived at the Embassy, we were surprised. The officials did not understand why David had spent the years he had in Mexico. Why had he left the U.S.? Who was he living with in Mexico? They refused to grant him a passport. I decided to return the next day and start again, this time with a different official. I was angry. The Embassy had a file on my case and knew that I had searched for them almost 13 years. Suddenly they had no concept what I was talking about? It was very frustrating.

The next day David and I returned again to the Embassy. This time I went up to the official who recognized me from the previous day. I repeated sternly that David had been abducted by his father and brought to Mexico where he had lived all these years. I showed the official the black book I had prepared for John M, the investigator who found the children, and all the supporting documents I had with me. I stated that I had a file with the Embassy and would like to talk with a supervisor. The supervisor arrived and along with the desk official at first did not want to grant him a passport. It was not until I said that I was not leaving the Embassy until we had David's passport that the supervisor then left and talked with his superior, who ultimately talked with me. They finally agreed to submit the paperwork so that David would have his passport. Unbelievable! It took hours. At the end David had an amazed and surprised look on his face. I said in Spanish, "No one messes with Mama Bear!"

Reflections

- Bring every piece of paperwork you can possibly think of including certified birth certificates, affidavits, statements from police in the U.S. and the foreign country. Bring proof of your residency in the U.S. (surprisingly a U.S. passport and driver's license is not good enough). Try to find out requirements before you go so you don't have to make multiple trips.

- In hindsight, I wish I'd obtained a copy of my Embassy file early on in my search and kept it for when I needed to get David's passport. It would have saved me time and frustration.

- Be persistent.

Appendix C: Resources for Families/ Volunteer Opportunities

There are a variety of national and international organizations that provide important information for families who have experienced child abductions and related crises. I have listed key organizations below. These groups offer excellent guidance, tips, and ideas. In addition, some of these organizations provide insights and guidelines on reunification when a family member has been recovered after a short-term or long-term separation. In addition to the support groups listed, most of the organizations offer volunteer opportunities.

National Center for Missing and Exploited Children (NCMEC)
www.missingkids.com

Child Find of America, Inc.
www.childfindofamerica.org

Child Quest International
www.childquest.org

Polly Klaas Foundation
www.pollyklaas.org

Find the Children
www.findthechildren.com

Association of Missing and Exploited Children's Organizations (AMECO)
www.amecoinc.org

Team HOPE (a support group for parents/families of missing and exploited children) and part of NCMEC
www.teamhope.org

Office of Juvenile Justice and Delinquency Prevention (OJJDP)
www.ojjdp.gov

U.S. Department of State
www.state.gov

National Crime Information Center (FBI)
http://www.fas.org/irp/agency/doj/fbi/is/ncic.htm

California Child Abduction Task Force
www.childabductions.org
Read "Reunification" – Georgia K. Hilgeman-Hammond, M.A., Retired Executive Director and Founder, Vanished Children's Alliance: http://www.childabductions.org/impact11.html

Redeeming the Family
www.redeemingthefamily.org

Parental Alienation Awareness Organization (PAAO)
www.parental-alienation-awareness.com

Appendix D: Combined Reflections

Reflections on Searching for your Children

- **Never go alone** – Find an ally that is not emotionally invested the way you are. Take them with you for support to meetings with law enforcement and any meetings with the other parent. Have plans in place for your safety and the children's.

- **Provide itinerary and detailed information to family and friends** – I never told my parents about the abduction until after I returned from the first trip. While I had legal matters/proceedings in action, e.g., scheduled meetings with my attorney in Mexico, initial documents to pursue divorce/custody, I neglected to disclose my trip plans with close friends and family members. If something had happened to me in Mexico, my family and friends would not have known where to begin to look for me or get help for me.

- **Resist magical thinking** – This is the hardest lesson because you are so broken-hearted and desperate, but a family abduction is very real and requires detailed planning and implementation to resolve. Being naïve is a form of denial. For me this was a way to survive the initial impact of my children being abducted, but it did not help me get them back and I put myself into dangerous situations.

- **Understand the abductor's agenda** – Abductors want you to go away and leave them alone with the children. Appealing to their better nature, trying to make them feel guilty or sorry for you or to even regret taking the children in the first place is naïve. These kids are theirs and they are entitled. You do not matter to the kids the way they do. Your planning and strategies will be more effective if you keep this in mind.

- **Understand what makes you/made you a perfect target** – There are common characteristics among abandoned spouses from before the abduction. Many were isolated and lonely when they met their spouse – perhaps living in another country like me. Many don't have strong family ties. This makes an ideal situation for abductors because they know the person left behind won't have a lot of support and resources to pursue the children. You will have to overcome these issues as part of the process of recovering your children.

- **Understand that a liar lies** – Carlos had lied to me repeatedly before and during our marriage, and yet I stayed with him. After he took the children he continued to lie me and I still hoped that he was telling me the truth! That was the desperate mother in me, but all it did for me was feed into the magical thinking.

- **Listen to outside perspectives** – I had friends, my bosses at work, my family and others all telling me that they did not trust Carlos to have my best interest at heart. I regret not listening to them. I regret that I was too defensive to see that they did have my best interests at heart.

- **Know you cannot change him/her** – This was a mistake I made in my marriage. I kept thinking he would change, that things would be different, that having a baby would make things different, or moving to Dallas would make things different. While this wishful fantasy is common in many relationships, it can be dangerous if you are dealing with deceitful, selfish and controlling behaviors. If your spouse is vain and prideful, if he/she seems indifferent to you, if his/her needs come before yours, you need to leave. He/she will not change.

- **Don't underestimate cultural issues** – I gave little weight to the cultural differences between the United States and Mexico. I had adjusted to living in Mexico, how hard would it be for Carlos to adjust to the U.S.? I was naïve enough to think he might even like it better! This was a bit of cultural prejudice on my part, and it meant I missed the big red flags that he would be going back to Mexico sooner rather than later.

- **Get counseling for yourself** – Carlos comes from a culture that sees counseling as a weakness, so I would have never gotten him to go; however, I strongly wish I had sought out counseling for myself long before he took the children. In the years since, I've worked through a lot of issues. Counseling has helped me survive the tough years without my children, the long search, and the dynamics of my first marriage so I didn't have to repeat them with my current husband. If your children have been abducted, don't try to go this alone! You need all the help you can get, including emotional support from a professional.

- **Get family support** – With some families this may not be possible, but if you can mend fences and rally the family around you, this is the time. Carlos had a fairly large family in Mexico which supported him in myriad ways from money to babysitting to helping him get a job to giving him a place to stay and much more. Plus there is all the emotional support a family provides. I did not have that kind of support for a long time so I had to build it. It makes a difference. I see a lot of situations where spouses have no money, no job, few resources and a distant family. They are not in a position to pursue the abductor financially or emotionally. This is a situation where family support can make a huge difference.

Reflections on Law Enforcement and Private Investigators

- **Do your homework** – I had experiences that would not have been necessary if I had done some investigating of my own ahead of time. Checking with the Better Business Bureau and State Licensing Bureaus is a good start, but it is essential to speak with previous clients about their experiences.

- **Beware of large fees** – A large fee is generally indicative of a scam. If they aren't willing to work with you on a per-hour basis or to have their fee tied to deliverables, then move on. While a modest retainer is reasonable to cover out-of-pocket expenses, $75,000 is not.

- **Look to law enforcement** – Investigators like Mike and John who are referred to you by ethical organizations and are driven by a passion to help. They are often more affordable than other practitioners.

- **Avoid magical thinking** – If someone is spinning you a story that sounds too good to be true…it probably is. Tracking down abducted children is hard work with lots of potential dead ends and disappointments along the way. You want confidence and competence in a PI but not promises that can't be kept. You also need to avoid magical thinking. Hiring a PI is not going to solve all your problems and bring your kids back right away. It can take a long time. Things can happen. My first investigator Salvador was planning his extraction when Carlos disappeared again. Setbacks like this are par for the course.

Reflections on Building Relationships

- **Focus on the long-term relationship –** It may not be the ideal or desired one, the importance is that there IS a relationship that continues to build.

- **Prepare to relive important childhood stages –** I learned from therapists that I consulted that children need to relive stages of their lives that they missed with the parent left behind – no matter how old they are when found. David, for example, went through his teenage period where he had to act out and rebel against mine and Earl's parental authority.

- **Accept what is and not what could have been –** Being real and authentic underscores acceptance of the actual situation. By erasing expectations, one lives in the moment and embraces each day. Calling life the new normal puts perspective into everyday activities. As difficult as it was for all of us when David lived with us, we were finally no longer visitors with each other, being on our best behavior. Superficiality was gone, the masks taken off, exposing who we really were. This is how families are – freckles, dimples, AND warts!

- **Be patient –** Don't push for the relationship to happen. It takes time to build trust, confidence, and love. I was so anxious for Monica's time with us to work out – that she would enjoy her semester at SMU so much that she would elect to transfer and graduate here and not return to Mexico. I was looking for the perfect ending. I looked more at what I wanted rather than what Monica desired and needed. In effect, my behavior pushed her to go back to Mexico.

- **Acknowledge their culture –** Children who have been raised in a foreign culture have that as their norm now. They need time to adjust to yours. The U.S. was new to Monica and David after so much time had elapsed. They each were listening and having to speak a new language, understand new cultural mores, geography, state and federal laws, etc. In both cases, Monica and David were also studying. While I understand the Mexican culture and speak the language, I was inconsistent in helping Monica and David adjust to a new way of life.

- **Plan to be disrupted –** When a child returns after a long-term separation, there is an adjustment for the parent/family too. In my case, Earl and I had not had children living with us since we had been together. What would it be like having an adult child live with us? It is challenging even for parents whose child had not been abducted. While parenthood often seems to be a natural instinct, on the job experiences are the true learning tools. Earl and I had to adjust to being parents, he as a stepparent, a role he had never experienced. As wonderful as it was to have Monica and David living with us, Earl and I also had to plan how we would continue to live our lives. We fell into some magical thinking about how wonderful it would be without some realistic planning about how challenging it could be.

- **Treat your returning child/children normally and consistently –** Being consistent with children as they adapt to the family is vital. Monica and particularly David would try to manipulate us, thinking that we would want to do everything possible to please in order for them to like us. Establishing and maintaining consistency in our parent roles while treating both as adults contributed to earning respect. Good old fashioned boundary setting is crucial to minimize manipulation.

- **Consider therapy for the whole family –** I am a strong advocate for therapy or counseling to grow and become healthier. Therapy has helped me immensely from when Monica and David were abducted, my search for them, and ever since I reunited with them. Earl has reached out for support too. I always advise parents who are reuniting with their children after an abduction to seek family counseling. It is immensely valuable to the process of rebuilding a family to sit down together with a professional.

  I learned this the hard way because I did not do so with Monica and David. We were not living together most of the time, which was part of the issue. The other problem was I focused on Monica and David and what I perceived as issues they had, rather than all of us as a family learning how to be a family again. I found a recommended therapist for Monica and she visited with this person a few times, but felt forced. She angrily wanted to know why she had to go. She was fine and did not need help. I learned a valuable lesson about my approach.

  Other families whom I've supported have found family therapy to be a huge help. Rebuilding becomes a family project to work on together. The focus is on getting to know each other and communicate rather than talk about the abduction (unless someone wants to).

- **Stay real –** To accept a relationship for what it is without unrealistic expectations is even more important now than in the early years after reuniting. As the relationship builds and expands, you might feel comfortable, so it is easy to fall back and think there will never be any more challenges/disappointment. Celebrate the successes and know that there will be ebbs and flows.

- **Go with the flow –** It is important to continually nurture the relationship and go with the flow while life's events occur. Both Monica and David are adults now and need to live their own lives. I do not possess them, I just want to participate and be a mother/friend in their lives.

- **Communicate** – One of the wonderful aspects of technology is that Monica, David, and I are able to text frequently. We connect. Even though we express that we love each other, send hugs and kisses, it is the thought behind the text that truly matters. We are thinking about each other when we communicate this way. Except for when we see each other in person and are able to truly converse, this communication reflects so often real feelings about what is happening in our lives. Even phone calls, while wonderful to hear each other's voices, are sometimes difficult. We seem hesitant to really talk. I don't know really why, yet I think I understand. Monica, I know, will call or I will call when she is at home. Since her father is living with her, I am never sure even at this point in her life how comfortable she is in talking about certain subjects. When we are together, she truly confides. David is more open. It does not bother him that someone is around although I can tell when he has a serious topic to discuss, he is not comfortable at times talking. I know then that someone is around he does not want to hear what he is saying.

- **Let go –** There will always be painful barriers in the relationship. I wasn't there when my children needed me, and they're angry about it. I took too long to find them. I died and then came back. I abandoned them (according to their father). The children have a lot of confusing and irrational feelings that must be addressed in a kind and loving way. It is not fair, but I had to drop my need to be right or to explain or to justify my actions in order to build a relationship with David and Monica. The shadow of Carlos lingers. He is Monica and David's father. His influence on them is still there and always will be. The key is to let go and accept what is. I love my children. Our relationship ultimately is what counts in my life.

- **Laugh –** A sense of humor will help you get through a lot of rough spots in the process. Laughing and having fun together helps with bonding. It also helps get through mistakes and awkward moments lightly. It is easy for things to become heavy pretty fast since there are a lot of big emotions at play. Joking and trying not to take things too seriously can help.

Reflections of a Stepparent

- Let your partner, the parent, do most of the talking. You are in a support role.

- Keep your mouth shut, listen and watch body language.

- Be a friend and just a friend.

- After you are a friend, you can start acting like a parent without being perceived to be an outsider.

- Use tough love if you have to, but remember you are the stepparent.

Reflections on Passports

- Bring every piece of paperwork you can possibly think of including certified birth certificates, affidavits, statements from police in the U.S. and the foreign country. Bring proof of your residency in the U.S. (surprisingly a U.S. passport and driver's license is not good enough). Try to find out requirements before you go so you don't have to make multiple trips.

- In hindsight, I wish I'd obtained a copy of my Embassy file early on in my search and kept it for when I needed to get David's passport. It would have saved me time and frustration.

- Be persistent.

About Susan Morrow

Acting as an advocate for missing children is Susan Morrow's personal passion and mission. She has supported families through the National Center for Missing and Exploited Children and Child Find of America. Ms. Morrow counsels families experiencing long-term abductions both in the U.S. and worldwide and provides post-reunification support.

Susan speaks to non-profit networking and advocacy groups as well as at conferences on the topics of missing children, family abduction awareness and prevention, victimization and empowerment and related subjects. She has also contributed her own personal story as a case study to technical journals and textbooks on the subject of family abduction and is one of four reviewers for a publication soon to be published by the Department of Justice's Office of Juvenile Justice and Delinquency Prevention (OJJDP) on the topic of parental abduction.

Additionally, she has 25+ years of experience in public relations/ communications and reputation management. She has planned and implemented programs for emerging and large businesses in diversified industries, including manufacturing, professional services, and retail. Ms. Morrow is a crisis management specialist and helps individuals and organizations in the areas of internal planning, communications with media, community, and industry organizations, and counseling during actual crisis situations.

Fluent in Spanish with a working knowledge of Italian and Portuguese, Ms. Morrow holds a Bachelor of Arts degree in English and Communications from Georgia State University and a Master of Arts degree in Developmental Psychology from the University of Saint Thomas, St. Paul, Minnesota.

Invite Susan to Speak to Your Group!

Long-Term Separation: No Strings Attached

- Reunification: expectations of a fairy-tale ending
- Familial alienation
- Attachment disorder
- Create and re-build personal and family identity

When a Stranger Returns: The Best Kept Secret

- Reunite with family members – prepare for an emotional roller coaster
- Navigate around a child's rejection and hostility
- Redefine normal and create a life together
- Experience the revolving door of disappointment
- Rebuild relationships: plan for long term success

My Country is Not Your Country: A Child's New Identity after a Long-Term International Abduction

- Accept a new culture, language and behavior
- Communication and integration between family members and child
- Bridge country and cultural divides to integrate family and child
- Confront non-acceptance by society

Giving Up, Going Under, Rising Above

- Self-destruct or self-empower when an unpredictable crisis occurs
- Creating a new life: the emotional dilemma
- Maintaining hope and positive perspective
- Take control of your life: benefits and rewards

International Child Abduction: Reality in Today's World

- Current research and findings
- Difficulties locating missing children in other countries
- Available international resources
- Prevention tips/guidelines for parents and families

Phone: 214-632-2711 · Email: smorrow@morrowpr.com
www.unbreakmyheart.com